The
Complete
Jean Vigo

Lorrimer Publishing

First printing 1983
SBN paper 0 85647 071 6
Distributed exclusively in the United States of America,
its territories, possessions, protectorates and places
mandated to it, the Philippines and the Dominion of
Canada by Frederick Ungar Publishing Company Incorporated,
250 Park Avenue South, New York, N.Y. 10003.

Phototypeset by *Sunrise Setting,* Torquay, Devon
Printed in Great Britain by Unwin Brothers Limited, Old Woking, Surrey

CONTENTS

ACKNOWLEDGEMENTS

Lorrimer Publishing wishes to thank Pierre Lherminier for his devotion and care in preparing the original *Ecrits de Jean Vigo* and the British Film Institute for its continuing concern with providing the facilities and archives for research and publishing books on the cinema. The front cover of the book is based on the original poster for *Zéro de Conduite*.

PREFACE

A PROPOS DE JEAN VIGO

I had the good fortune to discover all Jean Vigo's films in a single session one Saturday afternoon in 1946, at the Sèvres-Pathé cinema, thanks to the cineclub of *La Chambre Noire* which was run by André Bazin and other contributors to *La Revue du Cinéma*. I knew nothing of Jean Vigo at the time, not even his name, but I was instantly captivated by his work which, in its entirety, does not add up to more than 200 minutes. Although I was unaccustomed to seeing films made prior to 1942, I started out liking *Zéro de Conduite* better than *L'Atalante*, probably because I identified with the theme more. Later on, after seeing both films over and over again, I ended up definitively preferring *L'Atalante,* and it is one of the films that always springs to my mind when I must reply to questionnaires asking me which I think are the ten best films ever made.

Zéro de Conduite is more special than *L'Atalante* in one respect: it deals with the subject of childhood. Masterpieces on this theme, either in literature or films, can be counted on the fingers of one hand. Such works make a particularly strong impact on us, for they combine aesthetic enjoyment with personal recollections of a very intimate kind that stir our emotions. All films about childhood are evocative, since they take us back to the days when we wore short trousers, to the days of schools and blackboards, to the very *début* in our lives.

There is something experimental about *Zéro de Conduite*, as there is about almost every first film. A whole succession of ideas have been inserted into the script and shot just to 'try them out and see how well they'll work'. In the school celebration, for example, dummies mingle with real people on a platform which is also a fairground stand. This idea could come straight out of a René Clair film of the same period, and now looks old-fashioned.

1

But for every outdated experiment, there are at least nine fantastic inventions which may be droll, poetic or poignant, but which always remain visually potent and of a frankness which has never been equalled since.

When Vigo shot *L'Atalante* shortly afterwards, he had obviously learned a great deal from making *Zéro de Conduite*; in his second film, he attained perfection and made a masterpiece. He was still using slow-motion to achieve poetic effects, but he had given up using quick motion for comic effects and was no longer resorting to dummies. Only what was real now appeared before his camera, which effortlessly transformed reality into a magic vision, turning prose into poetry.

I am tempted to make a superficial comparison between the meteoric careers of Jean Vigo and Raymond Radiguet. Both artists died young, leaving only two works behind them. In both cases the first work is frankly autobiographical while the author appears more detached in the second because the actual subject has, in a sense, been imposed upon him from the outside. If we underestimated *L'Atalante* because it was commissioned, we would be forgetting that second works are almost invariably commissioned. Radiguet's *Le Bal du Comte d'Orgel* was commissioned by Cocteau, or its theme may have been self-imposed. The second work of an artist is, by definition, always significant: it will reveal whether he only has it in him to produce a single work and is just a gifted amateur, or whether he is a true creator; whether he is someone who happened to strike the right note once, or someone who is going to evolve and dedicate himself single-mindedly to the task of improving his talent. Vigo and Radiguet also evolved in the same fashion, going from realism and rebellion to preciosity and aestheticism (and I use both words in their most favourable connotation). There is no need to pursue the comparison between the author and the director any further, though we can still dream of the marvellous screen adaption Vigo could have made of *Le Diable au Corps*. We should also bear in mind the fact that when people have written about Vigo's works, they have consistently brought up the names of authors like Alain Fournier, Rimbaud and Céline, and always with good reason.

L'Atalante has all the good qualities of *Zéro de Conduite* and several others besides, such as maturity and control. It is a film which combines elements from the two great trends in the cinema: realism and aestheticism. In the history of the film, there have been great realists like Rossellini and great aesthetes like Eisenstein, but few directors have tried to mix the genres, as though for some reason they had to be kept apart. In my opinion, *L'Atalante* is like a mixture of *A Bout de Souffle* and *Nuits Blanches*, two splendid films which are at completely opposite poles, but which represent the very best of each style. The first film pieces together facets of the truth which add up to a kind of modern fairy-tale, while the second starts off as a modern fairy-tale through which we ultimately discover a universal truth.

L'Atalante is often underrated. I suspect this is because its subject is thought to be minor, dealing too much with a particular instance, as compared to the broader, more 'universal' theme of *Zéro de Conduite*. Yet the theme of *L'Atalante* is one which is not often handled on the screen: it is about the early stages of a young couple's life together and their problems adapting to each other. They start off happily enough, in the euphoria of their lovemaking, a stage which has been described by Maupassant as 'the brutal physical appetite which is so soon sated'. They have their first squabbles, begin to grow apart, eventually leave each other, then are reconciled and ultimately come to terms. If we see *L'Atalante* in this light, we soon realize that its theme is no less significant than that of *Zéro de Conduite*.

When we study the decade between 1930 and 1940, during which the first 'talkies' were being made, we discover that Vigo stood almost alone in the French cinema apart from Jean Renoir, the humanist, and Abel Gance, the visionary, though film historians do tend to underestimate the importance of Marcel Pagnol and Sacha Guitry. Vigo is much closer to Renoir than to Gance, but he is both more of a realist and more of an aesthete than Renoir. Both directors were brought up in similar circumstances: their childhood world was simultaneously wealthy and poor, working-class and aristocratic, but Renoir was not traumatised like Vigo. Renoir was the son of a celebrated painter and his chief problem was to do nothing unworthy of the name he bore; as we know, he came to the cinema after giving up ceramics because he found it too close to painting as an art form.

3

Vigo was also the son of a famous man, but of a very controversial one: his father, the anarchist leader, Miguel Almereyda, died while in prison, in mysterious and sinister circumstances. The orphaned child was sent to one boarding school after another, under a false name, and was so unhappy during these years that his later work still throbs with pain. An excellent biography of Vigo by P.E. Salès Gomès confirms, down to the last detail, everything one might suspect of Vigo's life after seeing his films. His great-grandfather, Bonaventura de Vigo, was a vine-grower in Andorra in 1882. Bonaventura's son, Eugène, died of tuberculosis at the age of twenty after siring Miguel. Aimée Salles, Miguel's mother, married a photographer from Sète called Gabriel Aubès; she later became insane and had to be confined to an asylum in 1901. Miguel adopted the name Almereyda because it sounded to him like the name of a Spanish grandee. He married Emily Cléro, a young anarchist who had already had five children by a previous union; all of them had died at an early age, one of them by falling out of a window. In 1905, she gave birth to Jean, whose life was destined to be so tragic and so short. When Almereyda died, Jean had little to call his own except for his great-grandfather's motto which could so easily be that of his droll and tender films: 'I protect the weakest'.

This motto also reminds us of one essential trait which Vigo and Renoir have in common: their passionate admiration for Charles Chaplin. Books on film history often overlook the chronology of various films and their influences on one another. Though I cannot prove it, I have always been convinced that Vigo was profoundly influenced by Renoir's *Tir au Flanc* (1928) when he made *Zéro de Conduite* in 1932. Like *Tir au Flanc*, Vigo's film is also divided up into set scenes punctuated by funny title cards: dormitory life, the school dining-hall, etc. *Tir au Flanc* itself had been directly influenced by Chaplin's films, especially by *Shoulder Arms* (1918). It is also more than likely that Vigo asked Michel Simon to act in *L'Atalante* because of the character Simon had created the previous year in Renoir's *Boudu Sauvé des Eaux*.

When I read the reminiscences of silent film-makers, I am usually struck by the fortuitous way in which they stumbled on their profession, completely by chance: maybe a friend had persuaded them to work as a film extra, or else an elderly uncle had taken them on a tour of a film studio. Jean Vigo is a total exception to this rule. He became a film director out of a sense of vocation and was one of the very first to make films solely for that reason. He started off as a filmgoer, and soon turned into a film addict, going to the cinema assiduously. He opened a film club just to bring the best films to Nice, and he felt the urge to try his hand at making films at an early stage. He wrote off to a number of people asking them for a job as assistant, adding that he was 'prepared to sweep up the actors' dung'. He then bought a camera and produced his first short film: *A Propos de Nice*.

It has often been pointed out that *Zéro de Conduite* is full of gaps; this is blamed on Vigo's extremely tight shooting schedule, but I think these gaps can also be explained by Vigo's urgent need to put across what he felt was most essential, and also by a young director's state of mind when he is finally given the opportunity to make his first film. He cannot quite believe it, it seems too good to be true. While he is making his film, he isn't sure that it will ever see the light of day. When he was just a filmgoer, he thought he could tell exactly what was good and what wasn't, but now that he has been entrusted with the job of making a film himself, he is filled with doubts and wonders if what he is doing won't be too unusual, too different from what is being made. He often ends up feeling his film will never be shown. This is why I suspect that when Vigo heard that *Zéro de Conduite* had been banned, he probably felt, after the first shock of disappointment, that the censors' decision merely confirmed his own worst fears. Perhaps he thought to himself: 'I always knew my film wasn't a proper film like the others'. Something of this self-doubt comes across in the speech of introduction which he made when *Zéro de Conduite* was shown in Brussels.

Jean Vigo may have been overcome by self-doubt, yet his first fifty metres of film, whether he realised it or not, established his reputation as a great director, the equal of Renoir, Gance or Buñuel, who was also just starting out on his career at the time. It is sometimes claimed that a man's character is formed between the age of seven and twelve. In the same way, it can also be said that a film director's entire career can be assessed from the first fifty metres of film he has shot. The essence of the man will be contained in that early footage and he will remain essentially true to himself from then on, though he may do better work (masterpieces) or lesser work (failures). The whole of Orson Welles is contained in the first reel of *Citizen Kane*, the whole of Buñuel in *Le Chien Andalou*, the whole of Godard in *Une Femme Coquette* (shot in 16 mm), just as the essence of Vigo's work is contained in *A Propos de Nice*.

Like all artists, film-makers set out trying to discover truth, whether through realism or through their own version of reality. They are usually tormented by the gaps which remains between what they were trying to achieve and what they actually did accomplish, between life as they feel it to be and life as they have succeeded in showing it. Personally, I feel that Vigo had very good reason to be more satisfied with his work than most artists, for he went further than almost any in recreating different facets of reality: the reality of inanimate objects, of an atmosphere, of people, of feelings, and above all the purely physical reality of life itself. In Vigo's case, one really can talk of an 'olfactory' cinema without exaggerating; this thought occurred to me when a journalist explained his extremely negative reactions to a film I was defending by declaring, as a final argument: 'And besides, that film stinks like a pair of dirty feet!' I did not reply at the time, but I later thought about this accusation and wondered if it wasn't just the way the censors had felt about *Zéro de Conduite* when they banned it. Salès Gomès described hostile reviews of the film which spoke of it as being 'like bidet water' and 'bordering on scatology.' André Bazin summed it up most accurately when he said in an article: 'Vigo is almost obscenely fascinated by the flesh'. And indeed, no one else has ever filmed such sheer *fleshiness* as authentically as Vigo. In fifty years of subsequent film-making, nothing has equalled that shot of the schoolmaster's plump hand pressing down on the child's small white hand in *Zéro de Conduite*, or the sensual way in which Dita Parlo and Jean Dasté cling to each other in *L'Atalante* when they are about to make love. An even more remarkable example in this film is the scene when, having left each other, they lie in different beds, Dasté in his barge, Parlo in her hotel room, both yearning for each other. This particular scene, which owes much to Maurice Jaubert's musical score, is nakedly sexual and at the

6

same time lyrical, while it undeniably shows us the act of lovemaking, though at a distance.

Both an aesthete and a realist, Vigo managed to sidestep all the pitfalls of aestheticism and realism in his films. He extricated himself from potential excesses in either genre by his lightness of touch in a scene like the one where Dita Parlo stands on the barge in the mist, wearing her wedding-dress, or at the other end of the scale, the scene in which Jean Dasté takes all his dirty laundry out of the wardrobe. He gets away with scenes of this kind because of his delicacy, his sense of humour, his elegance, his intelligence and his sensibility. What was his secret? Probably that he lived more intensely than most people. The cinema is a frustrating medium to work in because it is so full of stops and starts. You do a take of five to fifteen seconds, then you stop for an hour, so that you cannot work yourself into a fever of creation on a film the way certain writers, like Henry Miller for example, can at a writing desk. By the time a writer gets to the twentieth page, he is swept away by the creative urge and the words pour out onto the paper, making fantastic patterns. Vigo seems to have got through his work in this trance-like state, while remaining perfectly lucid at all times. He was already very ill during the shooting of both films and even had to direct certain sequences from a camp bed. Thus we can assume that he was quite literally 'in a fever' while he was filming and, as we know, this particular state can make a man more creative, more brilliant and more intense. When one of Vigo's friends advised him to take it easy, he replied that he felt his time was short and that he had to give as much of himself as he possibly could then and there. Knowing that he was doomed, Vigo strove to outdo himself; the limited time he had left goaded him on and made him feel, while he stood behind the camera, the way Ingmar Bergman once said every director ought to feel: 'One should make each film as though it were one's last'.

FRANÇOIS TRUFFAUT

BIOGRAPHICAL NOTES

Jean Vigo was born on 24 April, 1905, in the Rue Polonceau, Paris 18e. He was the son of two militant anarchists, Emily Cléro and Miguel Almereyda, whose real name was Eugène Bonaventura de Vigo. Almereyda came from a distinguished Andorran family, but had been rejected by his relatives for having been illegitimately conceived and the product of a *mésalliance*; he had lived in Paris since 1898 and had become involved in the Anarchist movement at an early age. After spending some time in prison, Almereyda had turned to journalism and was one of the founders of *La Guerre Sociale* (1906). He later became director of *Bonnet Rouge* (1913), a satirical weekly which became a daily in 1914. During the First World War, Almereyda's political leanings drew him into clandestine activities which have never been fully disclosed to this day. The outcome was the so-called *Bonnet Rouge* affair which led to Almereyda's arrest on August 6, 1917. He died in his prison cell at Fresnes during the night of the 13th in circumstances which have remained mysterious.

Jean Vigo grew up in an atmosphere of political activism; he was only twelve years old when his father died. He was taken to Montpellier in October of that year, where he lived with the Aubès family to which he was related on his father's side. He later attended school at Nimes after adopting his grandmother's name, Salles. Still known as Jean Salles, he went to boarding-school at Millau for the next four years. In October 1922, his mother, who had remained in Paris, asked for her son to be transferred to a *lycée* at Chartres under his real name. He left the *lycée* in July 1925 and entered the Sorbonne later that year.

Vigo was very interested in the cinema by this time and began seeing all his father's old friends in Paris. He idealised his father's memory and hoped to clear his name one day. At the beginning of 1926, he fell ill and went back to live in Montpellier. From there, he went to Font-Romeu in the mountains to try and restore his health. He arrived at Font-Romeu on 2 August and remained there for two years, leaving it only once for a few days at the end of December 1926. It was there that he met Claude Aveline, the author and publisher for whom he worked as a private secretary and who remained a loyal and helpful friend to the last. It was also at Font-Romeu that he met another young patient, a Polish girl called Elisabeth Lozinska, known to everyone as Lydou.

Vigo left for Paris with Lydou in November 1928, but they were advised to live in the South of France for reasons of health; so they left Paris for Nice in December, after making a few contacts with the film world. In Nice, Vigo found a little work at the Victorine studios. Lydou's father, Mr Lozinsky, came to Nice and helped them to set up house. He was present at their wedding, which took place on 24 January, 1929. Vigo wanted to make a film on Nice with his father-in-law's financial backing, and he began to make notes concerning this project. When he visited Paris during the autumn, he met Boris Kaufman, a film cameraman of Russian descent. He invited Kaufman to come down to Nice to make the film with him.

A Propos de Nice was shot between December 1929 and March 1930. It was first shown to the public on 28 May, at the Vieux Colombier in Paris. It was shown a second time on 14 June of that year and received a few good reviews in the press. Vigo met Charles Goldblatt on this occasion. When Vigo returned to Nice, he decided to try and start a film club in Nice; after spending some time in the mountains with Lydou during the summer months, the film club opened on 19 September; it was calles 'Les Amis du Cinema' and was inaugurated by Germaine Dulac.

Vigo went back to Paris at the beginning of October for the commercial release of *A Propos de Nice* at the Ursulines cinema, where it was given a favourable reception by the public. He met Albert Riéra and René Lefèvre, and tried to make further contacts in the film world. He was present at the shooting of some barge scenes in Jean Lods's film, *La Seine*, and later recalled these moments when he shot *L'Atalante*. At the end of

10

November, he attended the *Congrès du Cinéma Indépendent* at Brussels and was commissioned to make a short documentary for Gaumont – Franco – Film – Aubert. He shot the film *Taris, ou la Natation*, in January 1931 in Paris. He went back to Nice with his wife after the shooting, and his friend Henri Storck joined them there soon afterwards.

In March or April, they met Charles Chaplin who had stopped off at Nice on his grand tour of Europe. Storck, who was out of work, had to leave Nice in April. The Vigos too were in financial straits and Lydou was pregnant. The child, Luce, was born on 30 June and Lydou's father once again helped them out financially. Several film projects fell through during this time, and the Vigos went off to the mountains again during the summer months. At the end of November, Vigo left for Paris alone; there he wrote the script for *Cochet ou le Tennis* with Charles Goldblatt at the request of Gaumont – Franco – Film – Aubert. The project was accepted at first, then finally turned down in February 1932, although the film crew had already gone down to Monte Carlo and was about to start shooting.

Vigo then returned to Nice, where Storck and Storck's mother joined him in March. The film club started by Vigo was bringing in a little money and Mr Lozinsky was also contributing a small but regular income. The health of both Vigos was very precarious, especially Lydou's. The young couple returned to Paris at the end of April and stayed there until the end of May; they then returned to Nice in June, until they left for the mountains once again because of Lydou's health. They returned to Paris at the end of June and Lydou went from there to Leysin in Switzerland. Meanwhile, Vigo was still looking for work in the film world. In July, he was introduced by Lefèvre to Jacques Louis-Nounez, who was thinking of becoming a film producer. The two men studied various film projects and finally decided on a subject: *Les Cancres* (The Dunces), later known as *Zéro de Conduite,* drawn from Vigo's memories of his days at boarding-school. Vigo briefly joined Lydou at Leysin in September, and they returned to Paris in October where they found lodgings at 23 Rue Gazan, 14ᵉ, near the Parc Montsouris. Lydou's health had improved.

Shooting of *Zéro de Conduite* began in late December 1932,

and was completed at the end of March 1933, but it was refused distribution by the Censor. Despite this setback, Jacques Louis-Nounez decided to give Vigo a second chance and, during the following months, they studied various other film projects. By the end of August, Jacques Louis-Nounez had made his final choice: he wanted Vigo to direct *L'Atalante* and, after some hesitation, Vigo accepted. The film was shot between November 1933 and February 1934. After making a rough cut of the film, Vigo, whose health had greatly deteriorated during the shooting, spent a few weeks at Villard-de-Lans with his wife and a few friends.

When he returned to Paris at the end of march, Vigo had to take to his bed. He never left it again, growing more ill every day. He died in Paris, at the Rue Gazan, on 5 October, 1934. *L'Atalante,* which was now called *Le Chaland qui Passe*, was briefly shown in Paris during the month of September.

Lydou Vigo died on 24 April, 1939. Claude Aveline, Jean Vigo's executor, became the guardian of Luce.

L'Atalante was shown again in 1940, but it was not until 1945, when *Zéro de Conduite* was released for the first time, that Vigo's work received the full recognition which it deserved.

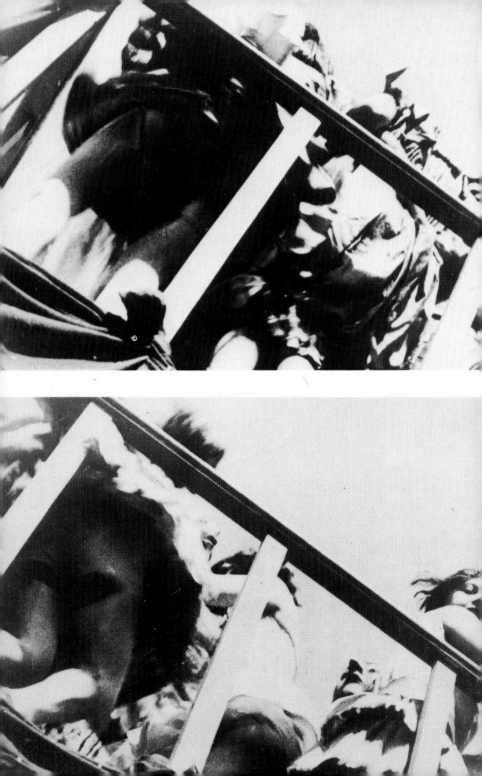

TOWARDS A SOCIAL CINEMA

(A speech delivered at the presentation of *A Propos de Nice*)

As you can imagine, we're not about to discover America. I hasten to say this so that you'll know right away, the exact meaning of the words printed on that scrap of paper you've been given and which promise you this and that.

Nor do I intend to explain in great detail what I mean by the social cinema, or to summarise the whole idea in one easy sentence. I'd just like to try to make you want to go and see good films more often, if our film-makers will allow me to use an expression like good in this context, in other words films which are about society and its impact on human beings and on inanimate objects.

You see, it's not that the cinema is wholly devoid of ideas, but that those ideas are usually wrong. The cinema constricts our brains the way the Chinese constrict their feet. Because it's still such a young art form, we're treated like babies. Films are just like daddies going 'kootchy-koo' to their brats.

Yet a camera isn't just a machine for creating a vacuum. A social cinema would involve us in the study of endlessly self-renewing topics drawn from everyday life.

It would liberate us from those two pairs of lips that take three metres of film to come together and almost that long again to come unstuck.

It would also free us from the extreme artistic subtlety of the so-called 'pure' cinema in which the director takes one shot after another of his navel, seen from this angle, that angle and yet another angle; technique for the sake of technique.

It would mean we could ignore the whole issue of whether the cinema ought to be silent, ought to have some sound or ought to be a 100% 'talkie', like our war disability pensions, whether it ought to be in colour, cinerama, aromarama, etc. ...

Because we wouldn't ask a writer, for example, to tell us if he used a goose quill or a fountain-pen to write his latest novel, would we?

Colour, sound, three dimensional effects, they're all like attractions at a fair.

And indeed, the cinema business is run just like a fairground.

A social cinema would basically mean saying something to people, which would awaken other reactions than just the burps of those who go to a movie because it's good for their digestion.

Maybe that way we'll avoid being given a magisterial spanking in public by Mr Georges Duhamel.

I wanted *Un Chien Andalou* to be projected here today because, although it describes an internal drama in poetic terms, I still think it has all the qualities of true social cinema.

Mr Buñuel has refused, however, for much the same reasons that I am showing you *A Propos de Nice* today and introducing it personally.

Yet, I'm sorry he refused. *Un Chien Andalou* is a very important work for all kinds of reasons. The directing is meticulous, the lighting skilful, the images and visual associations perfectly coherent, the dreams impeccably logical. It is a marvellous confrontation between the rational world and the subconscious.

I'm also particularly sorry because, considered as social cinema, *Un Chien Andalou* is the most courageous and lucid of all films.

May I add, if you don't mind me pointing it out, that these are rare qualities indeed in a film.

I've only met Luis Buñuel once, for about ten minutes, and we did not discuss the script of *Un Chien Andalou*. I can thus talk to you about it with an even greater freedom, as long as you remember that I am only expressing what is strictly my own point of view. Who knows, I may stumble onto the truth; whatever else, I'm bound to say a few foolish things as well.

To understand the meaning of the film's title, we have to remember that Mr Buñuel is Spanish.

An Andalusian dog is howling. Who's dead?

Our inertia is really put to the test: we accept all the horrors perpetrated by man, but we can't bear actually to see a woman's eye being sliced in two by a razor, on screen. Why should the sight be more horrific than that of a cloud scudding across a full moon?

Such is the film's prologue and we cannot be left unmoved by it. It is the guarantee that we shall see the rest of the film through different eyes, if I may put it that way.

Throughout the film, a steely hand holds us by the scruff of the neck and shakes us.

In the opening shot, we see an overgrown child cycling down a street, hands on hips, not holding the handlebars. That child, who wears bits of white cloth all over his body that flap like so many wings, is the living symbol of innocence in the process of being corrupted by its confrontation with the world which we accept the way it is (you get the world you deserve), a world of over-elaborate prejudices, of self-renunciations and of sad, romanticised regrets.

Mr Buñuel's blade is sharp indeed; it'll never stab you in the back.

A box for macabre ceremonies, for that final *toilette* of the soul when the body has long ceased to exist and is reduced to nothing more than a handful of dust nestling in the hollow of a bed.

A boot for the sadism which, in its most hidden form, amounts to nothing more than the casual curiosity of the bystander.

Now, let us tug at those ropes of morality that we tie round our necks. Let's have a look at what we're pulling.

A cork: that's a weighty argument.

A bowler hat: poor bourgeoisie.

Two priests: poor Christ?

Two grand pianos stuffed with carcasses and excrement: poor sensibility.

At last the donkey, in close-up: we were expecting that. Mr Buñuel is cruel.

Shame on those who, during their puberty, murdered the person they might have become, the one they search for everywhere, in the forest, along the beach where waves toss our

15

memories and regrets at our feet until nothing is left of them though Spring may return.

Cave Canem ... beware of the dog. It bites.

I express myself in this fashion to avoid making an arid shot by shot analysis of the film. You don't do that to a good film, you've got to respect its wildness, its poetry. I only wanted to urge you to go see *Un Chien Andalou* again, or to see it for the first time.

What does the social cinema amount to then? It basically consists of choosing authentic, really 'meaty' subjects, nothing else.

But I would like to tell you about a more specific category of social cinema which is more closely related to the sort of thing I am doing: the social documentary or, to be precise, the documented point of view.

In this unprospected domain, I can assure you that the camera is king, or, if not king, at least president of the republic.

I don't know if the result can be called a work of art, but I'm quite sure it's real cinema. Good cinema because no other art form, no scientific approach can take its place.

The gentleman making a social documentary is the fellow who is thin enough to slip through a keyhole to film Prince Carol in his nightshirt as he gets out of bed if, that is, the sight can be considered interesting in any way. The gentleman making a social documentary is the fellow who is small enough to slip into the high priest's throne at Monte Carlo, in other words the croupier's chair, which is no easy matter, believe me.

The great difference between a social documentary and an ordinary documentary or a newsreel is that the fellow who makes a social documentary clearly states his personal point of view and commits himself one way or the other, underlining his message to make it clearer, if needs be.

Even if the maker of such a film is denied the status of artist, at least he is an individual who is making a stand, which is worth something.

The camera must be focused on any subject which has value as a document; the material must also be considered as a document in the cutting room.

Needless to say, the characters appearing in such a film must not be acting; the camera has to catch them just as they are or else the film loses all value as a documentary.

The aim of the social documentary is achieved when it succeeds in revealing the hidden meaning of a gesture, when it shows up the hidden beauty or the grotesqueness of an ordinary-looking individual. The social documentary must lay bare the mechanism of society by showing it to us in its purely physical manifestations.

And it must do all this so forcefully that the world we once looked at with such indifference now appears to us in its essence, stripped of its falsehoods. The social documentary must rip the blinkers from our eyes.

A Propos de Nice is only a rough draft, a modest attempt at making a film of this kind. It indicts a type of society by showing us the salient features of a city's life. First the atmosphere of Nice is sketched in and the general spirit of the place, no different from many other places, unfortunately. Then the film gives a more generalised image of debased and absurd festivities which are like the last gasps of a society in its death throes. Such goings-on are nauseating enough to make one feel one would stop at nothing, not even revolution, to put an end to it all.

JEAN VIGO

17

A PROPOS DE NICE

(1929)

A PROPOS DE NICE*

Fireworks.

Fade in on aerial view of Nice: the city; *fade out:* the port; *fade out:* the seaside.

Fade in on the gaming-table, the roulette wheel, the green baize cloth with the croupier's rake raking in the chips.

Fade in on a desert landscape: sand, palm-trees, railway tracks. A toy train comes into shot and a toy couple get out of the train, to be instantly raked in by the croupier's rake like chips.

Fade in on shingle beach, the ocean waves.

Fade in on an aerial shot of the city.

Fade in on beach, waves.

Camera pans up the trunk of a palm-tree seen from below.

Fade in on waves.

Fade in on the legs of two dustmen sweeping the gutter in a street.

Fade in on the beach and waves.

A man trying to paint the nose of an enormous carnival figure.

A man wiping a table in a café.

A carnival figure for a float, seen from below.

A man putting up a parasol at a café table.

Cut back to the workshop where the carnival figures are being painted; a 'woman' glides majestically past the camera.

A waiter, carrying a stack of parasols on his shoulder, tosses them down one by one on the tables of a cafe.

Once again we return to the workshop and its carnival floats; someone is painting the teeth and lips of a mask.

A hand braids some palm-leaves.

* A Propos de Nice was made without a real shooting script, so that this is a shot-by-shot breakdown taken from the final version of the film itself.

21

A man cuts branches from a palm-tree; he is tied to the trunk by a belt.

Outlined against the sky, we see a palm-tree with its bare, straight trunk and its cluster of leaves at the top. *Camera pans down:* we see that it is a dwarf palm-tree in a pot.

Fade in on the trunk of a real palm-tree which is also potted and is standing in a garden. *Camera pans up,* this time, to reveal the top of the palm-tree.

The Grand Hotel de la Promenade, *shot at a 45° tilt, camera gradually returning to a horizontal position.*

Identical shots of the Palais de la Méditerranée and the Negresco.

Shot of a detail in a facade: a statue in a niche.

Fade in to tracking shot of the cracks in the pavement of the Promenade des Anglais; we see the shadow of a bench, of a balustrade.

Fade in on crowds of strollers.

Fade in on more strollers; shot of an old newspaper vendor in an invalid carriage. Shot of the carriage moving away; foreign newspapers are pinned all over its back.

Fade in on people sitting on various types of chairs.

Fade in on beach, rocks, sea.

Another shot of strollers. A man with a hat and cane, bowing; another man wearing dark glasses; a worker wearing a cap; a woman in a fur collar; a couple under a parasol; a seaside photographer.

Close up of a broom, a hand picking up papers and a dustbin on wheels.

A street hawker with a suitcase containing scarves; another hawker selling spectacles.

A woman dressed like a gipsy and carrying a baby is begging from two elegantly-dressed ladies sitting on chairs; the ladies look away.

The camera rises to show us the promenade, seen from above, then the beach and the sea, on which we can see two hydroplanes; one of them is taking off.

Promenade, strollers, beach.

Hydroplane.

Sails of boats. A yacht race.

Dissolve to a tennis player serving a ball.

Sailing-boats.

Tennis player.

Sailing-boats.

The tennis player's legs, then *full shot* of him.

Shot of spectators at a tennis match.

The tennis player, who is wearing an eyeshade, leaps up into the air.

Spectators.

Alternate shots of both tennis players.

Spectators.

Players.

A bowl rolling towards camera.

Tennis player,

The bowl again in *close up*.

And the player in a game of bowls, throwing his bowl.

Shot of players during a game of bowls and shot of the bowls.

Dissolve to: a racing-car on a track.

Then shot of a buoy in the water.

Sailing-boats.

Racing-car.

Sailing-boats.

Racing-car.

Sailing-boats and wake left by water-skier.

Expensive car pulling up in front of a carpet rolled out on pavement; a fashionably-dressed woman steps out of the car.

A second car, seen from above, pulls up at the same spot and a chauffeur gets out to open the door for another elegant woman.

A bearded gentleman sitting at the terrace of a café.

A young woman wearing a hat turns away from camera until her face is hidden by the hat.

The man makes a little sign.

The young woman slowly turns to show her face again and even gives a little smile.

Café terrace: a man looks at the woman who sits at the next table, chatting. Another man drinks.

A woman strolling under a parasol.

A man walks a dog which is wearing an enormous bow round its neck.

An old lady, elegantly dressed, wearing a fur collar.

Rapid dissolve to: the head and scrawny neck of an ostrich.

A woman carrying flowers and a parasol.

A seated lady with a parasol.

Another lady reading a newspaper through a lorgnette.

More men and women reading newspapers.

Corner of the beach with birds.

A man asleep on a chair.

Another man, resting his head on his hand.

A couple of street entertainers with a big drum and an accordion. The drum has a negro's face painted on it.

A man sitting in the sun, fast asleep.

A violin.

Another sleeping man.

A woman playing a harp.

A man asleep.

A bearded man with a newspaper over his head.

A young woman's legs.

A man's feet.

Another woman's legs.

A seated man.

A woman arranging her stocking.

A woman sitting with crossed legs.

A man who seems to be turning his head abruptly to stare at ...... the legs of a woman reading a paper; her knees are tightly pressed together, her feet wide apart.

A warmly-dressed young woman, seated; she is wearing a coat.

Fade in: the same, wearing a summer dress.

Fade in: the same, wearing a longer dress.

Fade in: the same, wearing an open-necked, sleeveless white dress.

Fade in: The same, wearing a less revealing black dress.

Fade in: the same, naked.

Dissolve to: naked statues adorning the facade of a building on the Promenade.

Beach. A bather dries himself in front of a beach-tent.

Woman sitting on a deck-chair in the sun, a handkerchief over her eyes.

Bathers in the sea; two men are tossing a ball.

Women in bathing-suits sitting in deck chairs.

An old man who has turned up his trousers so that his legs are bare to the knee.

Another old man wearing a little sailor's cap, sunning his face which is screwed up in a grimace.

Fade in on his sunburnt face.

Dissolve to a group of crocodiles sunning themselves by the waterside.

The facade of the Palais de la Méditerranée, seen from below. The camera travels along the facade, following its sinuosities, its arches.

Dissolve to the thin strip of sky which shows above the old houses in one of the narrow streets of the *Vieux Nice*. Laundry drying on a line.

Camera pans down the facades of the houses to a public wash-house; we can see women and heaps of laundry.

Another shot of the laundry drying on lines strung from windows, seen from below.

Camera travels across the old house-fronts, the alleys.

Tilt down to two cones which are just like giant coolie hats; in fact, they are baskets which two boys are carrying on their heads.

A group of children, playing. Shot of their hands. *Tilt down to* their game.

A woman with a huge basket on her head; it contains dough which she is taking to the baking-oven.

Shot of the market.

Dough cut into strips.

Children at play. Their hands, faces.

Close up of child's face.

Gutter, garbage; a cat stares into camera and runs away.

Dissolve to the feet of people dancing; they are wearing evening dress and are at a fashionable nightclub.

Shots of couples dancing, either smiling into camera, seen from the back or seen from below, alternating with shots of people sitting at tables, drinking.

Fade in on shot, very out of focus, of carnival floats on parade, accompanied by throngs of people.

A ring of dancers wearing fancy-dress.

Young girls on a float, throwing flowers.
Orchestra.
Grandstand.
Float with girls throwing flowers.
Procession of enormous heads.
Close up of dancing 'bear.'
Floats, battle of flowers.
Face of an old woman in a hat as she gets pelted with flowers and tosses them back.
Ground littered with flowers.
Fade in on women picking flowers in a field.
Cut back to the city pavement, littered with crushed, soiled flowers.
A man picks up flowers to throw them.
Other people hurling flowers.
A float with gigantic insect wings.
A dog in the crowd picks up a flower in its mouth.
A policeman gives two children some flowers.
Various carnival figures, seen from below: men dressed as cats, as giant heads, as musical instruments.
A group of women and transvestites dancing on a float.
Orchestra.
Naked legs of dancers on a float, throwing confetti.
Dolls in a shop window with superimposed reflection of the plate glass.
Confetti vendors.
Confetti battle; floats.
Dancers on float; *slow motion shot* of their legs, seen from below.
Decorations strung up across a street.
A group of 'penguins' and another group of 'negresses' marching down the street.
Dissolve to an old officer astride a horse.
Close up of someone wearing a mask.
A military procession, seen from above; soldiers doing the goose-step.
A cross in a cemetery.
A brass band.
Dancers on a float.

Very rapid sideways pan to: a fleet of battleships at anchor in the harbour.

Shot of dancers, then *hold on* the warships.

Two policemen.

A priest, seen from above, walks past a poster, stops to look at it, then crosses the street.

Camera tilts down on a hearse, followed by a crowd of mourners, going past in quick motion.

Orchestra.

Statues of angels in a cemetery.

An old woman throwing flowers and confetti.

An invalid's wheelchair.

Faces of men and animals: an ox, a mule.

A porter with several decorations pinned to his chest greets a bootblack.

Fade in on the bootblack who is busily polishing a pair of naked feet.

Close up of the military medals on the porter's chest.

Crosses in a cemetery.

Strollers, shot from below.

A chimney.

People stepping over an open manhole, seen from below.

Statues of angels in a cemetery: a bust (when we see it from the back we realise it is hollow). Tombstones, very ornate tombs: *bas relief* of a mother and father standing on either side of medallions containing portraits of two children; *mater dolorosa*.

Cloudy sky.

Ocean waves on a beach.

Palm-trees.

The statue of a *mater dolorosa* in a cemetery.

An athlete showing off his abdominal muscles.

Cut back to a statue in the cemetery.

Cloudy sky.

The sea and waves.

Close up of a perforated rock through which we can see rays of sunshine.

Trees blowing in the wind.

The faces of old women, chattering to each other, seen from below.

27

Factory chimneys, shot from below.
Faces.
Chimneys.
Faces.
Chimneys.
Grotesque faces, like caricatures, horribly made up and grimacing.
Camera tracks down into an open tomb in the cemetery.
An old woman's face.
A cardboard figure from a float, lying on its side.
A chimney belching black smoke.
Two workers talking together.
A chimney belching white smoke.
Chimneys, seen from below.
A furnace at a foundry.
Chimney and smoke.

END

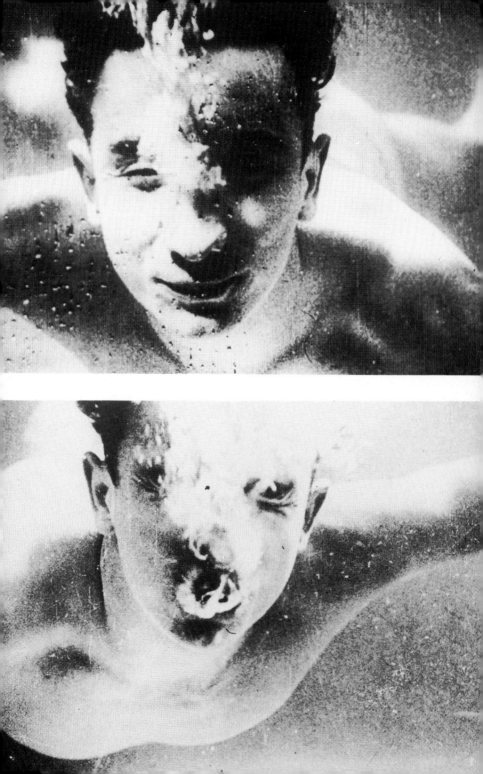

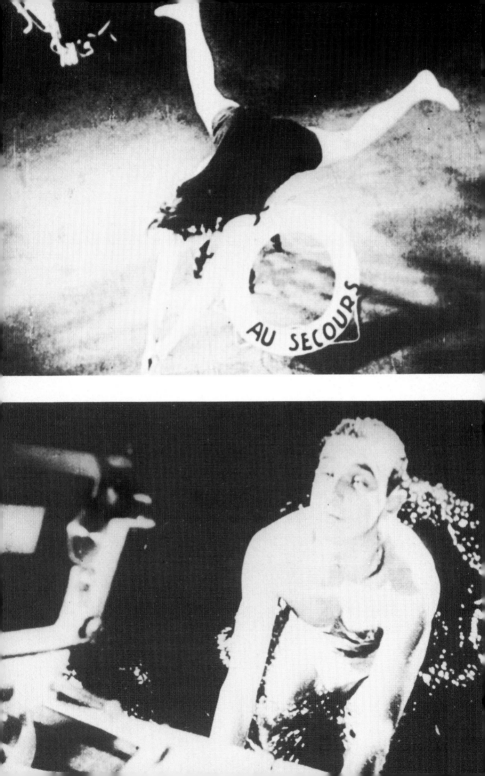

TARIS OU LA NATATION

(1931)

NOTES FOR THE FILM ON TARIS SWIMMING*

Jean Taris was born in Versailles, on 6 July 1909. When he was eight years old, his father taught him how to swim. In 1924, aged fifteen, Taris saw some of the American swimmers who had come to France for the Olympic Games and were performing at the Bain des Pages in Versailles-Trianon. Taris was particularly impressed by the swimming style of Johnny Weissmuller.

The boy started to train at the Bain des Pages under the supervision of Messier, the swimming instructor, who was his first real coach. In 1925, he won a swimming competition at the *Concours de l'Auto*, at the Hôtel de Ville swimming baths.

Taris, now a student at the Lycée Michelet in Vanves, went to the S.C.U.F. with some of his friends and met Hermant there. Hermant became his second coach, with whom he trained every Thursday.

TRAINING:
You train in the following way: studying leg movements, body positions, shoulder movements (shots of these movements to demonstrate the various positions).

In the shoulder movements, make a particular study of the way the arms move in the water (shots to demonstrate movements).

BREATHING:
To begin with, the young athlete draws in his breath at every stroke (demonstrate with photos). At a later stage, however, in order to gain speed he breathes in only at every stroke and a half.

SWIMMING STROKE:
He starts out with the breast stroke, to relax his muscles, then proceeds to the crawl (sprint).

* These notes, under the above headings, were found in Jean Vigo's papers. They are dated 10 November 1930.

DEPARTURE:
Show the swimmer standing by the edge of the pool, about to dive into the water.

SHARP TURN:
Show the swimmer making several sharp bends each time he reaches one end of the pool.

BACK STROKE:
Show swimmer doing various back-stroke exercises.

TRAINING:
Taris now spends at least one hour a day in training. Show him during training session for 300 to 1500 metres. Show his leg movements, his shoulder movements, his final sprints when he reaches the end.

SPORTING CAREER:
At first, all his friends at the S.C.U.F. performed better than he did.

In November 1926, fifth in a relay race, he won the Roland Levy challenge.

In 1927, he won three Paris championships: the 200, 400 and 1500 metre races.

That same year, he won his first international victory against the English Champion, Peter, in the 800 metre race.

It was also in 1927 that Taris won three French championships: the 200, 400 and 1500 metre races.

He was in the finals of the 1500 metre race in the European Championship.

In 1928 (year of the Olympics), he was consistently beaten by Vanderplancke throughout the year, except in the 1500 metre race.

In November 1928, he started training again with Hermant and won two international races in Belgium, the 200 and the 400 metre races, finally defeating Vandeplancke. Came last in the 1500 metre Olympic race.

Taris beat 23 French records in all swimming distances in 1929. Since that time, he has held all the 100 to 1500 metre records. He defeated the German champion, Rademacker, in the 400 metre race, beating the 1924 Olympic record of Weissmuller during this race. He beat the German champion, Derichs, in the 100 and 200 metre race. Was in turn beaten by Barany in the 100 metre race at the Grand Prix de Paris. Won every French championship in freestyle: 100, 200, 400 and 1500 metres.

Was both champion and record-holder at distances in England of 500 and 880 yards.

Tried to beat the 880 yard world record in 1930, but failed by one-fifth of a second. Established a new world record for 800 metres which he still holds. Beat the Italian champion, Costoli, in the 400 metre race and came within seven-tenths of a second of beating the world record. Beat the Hungarian, Barany, in the 200 metre race and beat the European record on this occasion. Was beaten by Barany in the 100 metre race, but won all four French championships.

ZERO DE CONDUITE

(1933)

SENSITIVITY OF FILM

(Written by Jean Vigo for the Brussels magazine *Sesame,*
1 December, 1932)

At this stage of 'Scientific Progress', man's eye is as insensitive as
his heart.

This would be a depressing thought if we did not have some
good reasons for having faith in the cinema.

We must not be put off if the latest commercial ventures are
labelled 'hypersensitive'. Let us recall the use made of the term
'spectacular', which was once the ultimate accolade in the film
world, the OK of OKs.* Our colleagues who own the film
equipment and the cinemas may deliberately allow themselves to
be misled by false descriptions so as to make a profit, just as film-
goers may accept misleading labels out of inertia, mysticism or
suicidal tendencies; but this must not allow you to be taken in,
disinterested experts of the laboratory who wish to pursue your
experiments without any preconceived notions. You will not be
fooled, any more than you were by that esteemed colleague of
yours who gave his dog a permanent wave and then insisted that
it was a poodle.

And it is you, the genuine benefactors of the cinema, who must
come to our rescue.

S.O.S.!

You who don't yet know that the cinema is a great Art, that the
cinema is Life, that the cinema is Vital.

No, I haven't forgotten that you gave up the first sweet,
epileptic images of C.I.N.E.M.A.T.O.G.R.A.P.H.Y, and that
you were extremely stoical about giving up slow motion and

* *Vigo's note:* OK: an American expression used exclusively by French
film directors to mean OK.

other tricks of that sort to save us from 'pure cinema'. Didn't you, only recently, carefully avoid the temptation of showing us nothing but speech-makers and opera singers when the talkies came in?

And I'm also convinced that your colour films won't contain artificial tints, that you'll go easy on the three dimensional effects and that your television too will be sensible.

...... But of course I'm forgetting that we've lost faith in the cinema as a potential art form.

Aren't we always making comparisons between the theatre and the cinema? Don't we refer to this or that painter whenever we see certain images on the screen? Don't we bring up the subject of music and musicians as soon as we start discussing sound effects? We examine a film shot the way we would read a page in an novel, as though the celluloid film were nothing but a sort of transparent map.

We've been saying that the cinema is in its infancy for so long that we've all turned into old men in the process.

And there's only one way an old man can make money: that's by gambling. What are the odds? Whatever they are, they're against the film directors.

They're for the unknown troglodytes of the test-tubes. Though I admit both categories have their part to play in the making of any film.

But I'm now being obscure. Who wants to lay a bet? The odds are to be against Film People. They are to be for the Revelation contained within the Image that is imposed on us, almost by chance, by human catalysts, if I may use this current expression.

So let us give up here, as in other domains, our fancied superiority over matter, over the machine.

Let us stop claiming that this or that film director, actor or producer is going to, at last ... At last what? Just when film reviewers, who grow more cocky every day, are making advance publicity so very expensive.

Let us instead be like auxiliaries; as we must earn a living in these hard times, let us do so as qualified technicians.

These qualified technicians would be like the negro porters

who make a direct contribution with their toil to what may well be a magnificent undertaking, while remaining wholly ignorant of its scope.

Our mission would consist of transporting cameras and film equipment to any spot where something was happening. Perhaps the hardest part of our work would be remembering to go and fetch the cameras once the action was over, so totally absorbed would we have become in our drinks at the local *bistro*.

This was my train of thought one very dark evening in Paris, on 2 September, 1932. I was standing in front of the Salle Bullier where a delegation had come to report on the activities of the World Anti-War congress, chaired by Romain Rolland, which had taken place in Amsterdam a few days earlier. Maxim Gorki, Willy Munizenberg, Marcel Cachin, Schwernik and Henri Barbusse, among others, were members of the delegation. 25 000 people had turned up to hear them, and there was only room for 7 000 inside the hall.

The street was full of people who were there out of curiosity or conviction. It was a calm, silent, somewhat melancholy gathering, a crowd waiting, hemmed in by policemen on all sides.

At 9.00 o'clock, a whistle blew. Orders had been given to charge.

Rearing on their horses, sabres raised, the mounted police charged into the crowd. So did the special brigade in which France's best athletes are to be found. So did the helmeted mobile policemen. Out came the truncheons, which aren't eggplants, but made of real wood, the kind you burn to keep warm, the kind which can crack open a skull in one blow. Fists crashed down on noses which broke under the impact. Eyes were gouged out and dangled from the optic nerve like our grandfathers' watches from their chains. Both men and women received many a Freudian kick below the belt.

'Get a move on!'

9.15 p.m.

'Stop! Make a body count.' No dead among the demonstrators, no wounded in the ranks of our police force.

And only the dim gas-lamps to light up this urban scene!

When, oh when, will the film itself grow photosensitive to sights of this kind, as men themselves refuse to care?

JEAN VIGO

INTRODUCING ZERO DE CONDUITE

(A speech delivered at the first showing of the film in Belgium on
17 October, 1933)

I am somewhat startled to find myself standing on this platform
all alone.

Given the spirit in which we made *Zéro de Conduite*, it would
have been more appropriate if the film had been introduced to
you by the entire team. I would then have bowed to you, like a
chorus girl, one of a line with all my collaborators, and that
introduction, however brief, would have been worth more than
any number of mumbled words.

I also think I ought to have brought a few members of the Film
Board of Censors since they cut a film about so much that they
often end up being its true authors; but I didn't want those
gentlemen to get bruised on the journey.

So I'll just pay a brief tribute to them instead, since they are
such fervant admirers of *Zéro de Conduite*.

'You know,' they told me, smacking their lips, 'we love it so
much we can't bear the idea of anyone else seeing it.'

What touching possessiveness!

You must admit it would be wrong for me to complain. All I
can hold against them is that they are being a trifle selfish,
however excellent their judgement.

Perhaps you all believed until tonight that my film had been
banned for other, less worthy motives; perhaps because the
censors found it 'anti-French' in spirit, whatever that means. Not
that it was ever stated explicitly since the Board of Censors never
has to explain its decisions; but it was generally thought that this
was the true reason, though everyone who has seen the film in
France is astonished such a pretext could possibly be invoked. I

41

also might well tell you that the President of the Board of Censors told one of his friends, who went to see him privately concerning the film veto, that he and his colleagues had been given unofficial orders by the government to ban the film before they had even seen it or had the opportunity to make up their minds for themselves.

No, you shouldn't believe everything you hear. That's why I'm here to dispel any false ideas you may have about the film.

I'm convinced it will get passed some day.

Just imagine: the whole film has been banned. Not just bits of it, but *all* of it.

Does this mean that our Board of Censors lacks discrimination? Surely they could have selected a few metres here and there that were innocuous, a few scenes that could be shown to the public without actually setting off a riot?

Could it be that the sole mission of the Board of Censors is to sabotage the independent film industry, to scare off the last few capitalists who are still ready, however reluctantly, to invest some of their money in certain film ventures?

I begin to wonder if those supervisors of artistic morality aren't serving heaven knows what commercial interests or shady opportunistic policies? Wouldn't that explain why some great Russian films which were banned outright two years ago are now getting passed in their uncut, original versions? Let us recall how, only a few months ago, a Soviet documentary did not get passed because the young Russians in it looked too happy and healthy and different from the usual stories we hear of abandoned kids growing up wild in every red nook and cranny of Russia, kids who eat grown-ups without a qualm whenever they can get their hands on one. And now, we're entitled to listen to the *Internationale* being played from start to finish every week at all the Pathé-Nathan cinemas.

No, I tell you, you mustn't believe everything you're told.

Are we to assume that the peace-loving but watchful sentries, who guard our obsolete and hypocritical institutions, cannot see beyond the points of their bayonets because they are completely blindfolded by the tricolour flag? That they are terrified of any reference to France and all things French, being scared of that alone and of nothing else. Really, if we believed that we would be forced to conclude that every administrator, policeman, bureaucrat and pen-pusher was a fool, which would be arrogance on our part.

I deliberately made *Zéro de Conduite* a realistic film. What I did was to set down my childhood recollections and if, in the process, I added a touch of satire here and there, I still don't see why the French government felt so threatened, why it had to blow its nose so loudly if my film made it sneeze. There isn't much point in being satirical about this or that government, this or that country, since all of them are basically alike apart from one.

I had no intention of taking you on a guided tour round a society in decay, like those Cook's Tour guides who show tourists round disease-ridden alleys in picturesque slums.

No, my purpose was more solemn. My preoccupation was more universal and disinterested.

Childhood. Kids abandoned every autumn in provincial boarding-schools all over the world. Kids who live far from the homes where, we hope, they might have known a mother's love, a father's companionship, if they still had a father.

At this point, I feel terribly worried. You're about to see *Zéro de Conduite* and I'll be seeing it again with you. I saw it at every stage of its development and now it looks so puny to me, so sickly! More like my offspring than like my own childhood, however hard I try to see it with the eyes of love. My childhood memories have somehow got lost in it. Did it all really happen so long ago? How could I have left my old school pals behind? How could I just grow up and set off on my own down the path followed by Le Grand Meaulnes? Of course, I recognise those two pals in that train compartment when the summer holidays are over. And I also recognise that dormitory of my eight years as a border, with those thirty identical beds. I can also see Huguet, whom we were so fond of, his colleague, *Pète-Sec*, and that silent supervisor who crept around like a ghost in crêpe-soled shoes. And that little sleep-walker, lit only by the gas flame of a night-lamp, will he come back to haunt me in my sleep tonight? Will I see him again, standing at the foot of my bed just as he did the

43

night before he died of Spanish flu in 1919? His coffin was taken down to the main courtyard and sprinkled with holy water by a priest to cast out the Devil who terrified us all.

Yes, I know, my pals, Caussat, Bruel, Colin, the cook's son, and Tabard whom we all called 'the girl,' Tabard who was spied on and persecuted by the school administration when all he really needed was a big brother since his mummy didn't love him.

I also recall that little girl whom I used to go and visit very occasionally on Sunday. Do you remember how I liked to look at you as you climbed onto the piano to unhook the goldfish bowl we had strung up on a wire together, our hands touching as we did so?

You saw me staring at your plump, baby's thighs and you covered my eyes with a handkerchief that smelled sweetly of your mother's *eau de cologne*. Then you took away the handkerchief, as gently as if you were removing a bandage from a wound, and we both gazed in silence at the goldfish in their bowl.

How well-behaved one had to be just to be allowed out for a few hours every Sunday!

I've shown the dining-room, where we ate all those beans, the classroom where, one day, a boy twice said, in a loud clear voice, what we all secretly thought.

I've shown you the plot we cooked up and took such trouble over at night in the loft, the plot which created such chaos! I've shown you how we crucified *Pète-Sec*, how we disrupted the official festivities which took place on that appropriately-named day of Sainte-Barbe.*

Will I ever set off across those roofs once again, towards a better world, slipping out by that loft which was the only place we could call our own?

Well, no, I didn't capture what it was really like. I failed and now I plead guilty before I finish this speech.

I am totally responsible for this failure and it really makes me sad not to be offering you a better film when the subject-matter is so very close to my heart.

But I won't make any excuses for myself.

A director doesn't have the right to go before the public and

---

* *Barbe* – a pun on the name of this woman saint and the slang word 'barber' which means both annoyance and boredom.

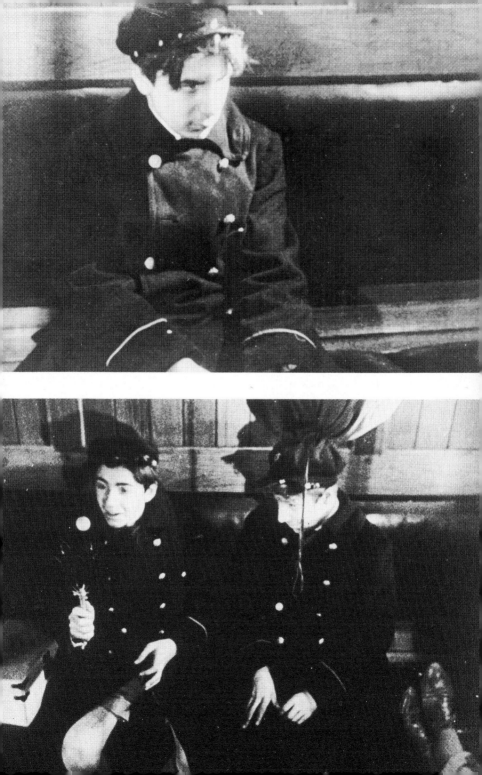

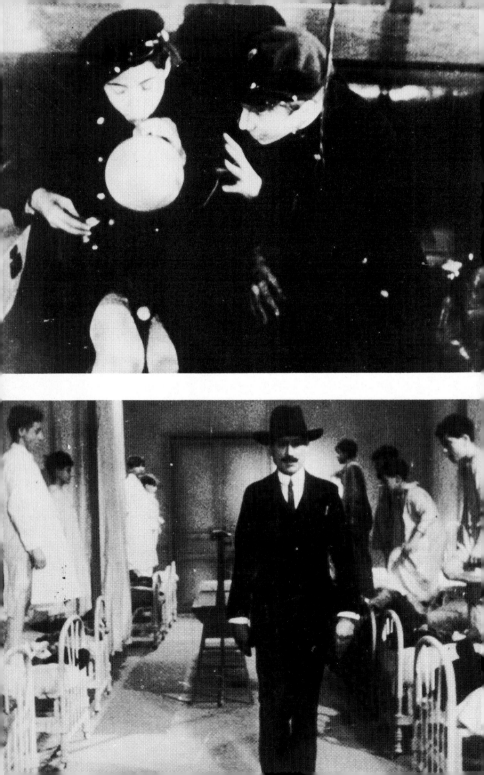

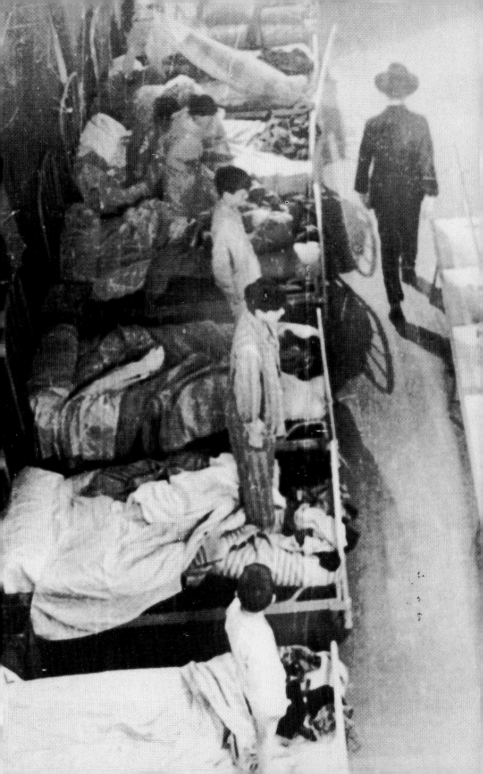

make excuses for the flaws in his film, blaming his partial or total failure on other people or on circumstances.

Freedom! I wasn't free to express my ideas as I really intended to express them.

Then why did you choose that particular format? In this bourgeois society we live in, the film director is like a kind of foreign body within an organism solely geared to make money according to a set formula which is dictated by the demands of the market.

However paradoxical it may seem, the film studio's ideal would be to produce only one film which would go on making money forever. Many top studios hire film directors year after year to do nothing, begging them just to go on fishing trips for an indefinite length of time.

When the occasional film does get made, it is processed and packaged like some rather unappetising food item: the only way to sell it is to lie about it on the label. Those tin containers in which film-reels are kept could well come out of a trick shop: who knows, you might find a talking bean inside one of them instead of a sound movie!

We know that from the start. If we don't like it, we are free to go and sell noodles instead!

No false excuses either! We're not allowed to cry out: 'But the censors ruined my film by cutting it about! Just look at the results!' On 4 October, 1933, there was a shameful little item on the back pages of the newspapers. It had deliberately been made almost illegible through misprints which the typographers had been ordered to make and it read:

> 'An agreement has been reached between Mr de Monzier and Mr Camille Chautemps whereby the Film Board of Censors is to be transferred from the Ministry of Education to the Ministry of the Interior'.

Hurrah! This official decision is a first step towards honest, if cynical, State Censorship. From now on, let every film-maker go and have his fingerprints taken at the police-station; let him confess all his cinematographic crimes; let photographs be taken of him from all three angles, as is done with common criminals; and let him, if need be, go and take a brief rest in the

Spontaneous Confessions chamber.

I'm not telling you anything you don't already know.

The one excuse a film director's not allowed is shouting at the top of his voice: 'My producer is an idiot!' Please, we reply, you're not making a documentary now.

Of course, we've heard of one film producer who insists on having the flag raised over the studio whenever he deigns to set foot there.

So what? Is your film making money? Have you been asked to make another? Will your next film be a failure just like this one? It will? Right. Then shut up and admit that you alone are to blame.

That's all I would like you to remember about this speech of mine which has gone on far too long. Here stands the culprit. His accomplices are all behind him. No one and nothing interfered with our work. Yet the film, all 1200 metres of it, is full of flaws as you are about to see. I worry about it and beg your forgiveness as I would that of a friend on whom I'd played a nasty practical joke.

JEAN VIGO

ZERO DE CONDUITE

(1933)

ZERO DE CONDUITE

(Nought For Conduct)

During the credits, we hear schoolboys singing in chorus, then the noise of a train. Before the opening shot, the following insert:

'THE HOLIDAYS ARE OVER
BACK-TO-SCHOOL DAY'

A THIRD CLASS COMPARTMENT — NIGHT

Close-up of the door of a third class compartment without a corridor. It is night. The light from the oil lamp is extremely dim and flickering. The smoke from the engine mingles with the fog. There is an occasional glimmer of light outside. A succession of flashing lights can be seen outside the half-open window of the compartment door.

A schoolboy of about twelve, wearing a cap and a greatcoat, sits towards the centre of the compartment. He is quiet, pensive, maybe a little worried or even a trifle sad. His name is GEORGES CAUSSAT *(a child who keeps to himself in the company of other children). We hear the monotonous sound made by the moving train.* CAUSSAT, *his head slightly drooping, is looking towards the right (another quick shot of the compartment door) and then to the left ....*

Shot of a man, his hat pulled down over his eyes to keep out the glare. He is asleep in one of the corner seats opposite the boy. Long shot of the compartment: the two occupants seen in profile. In the background, the engine smoke rushing past the window.

CAUSSAT, *who was being so quiet until now, starts to grow*

*increasingly restless as the train approaches a town, where it
will probably stop. (A sudden ringing sound, which almost
immediately grows fainter, tells us that the train has just passed
a level-crossing.)*
CAUSSAT *gets up and presses his face to the window (quick shot
of him seen from the outside, slightly from below).*
*The train pulls in at the station and as it comes to a halt (we are
again inside the compartment)* CAUSSAT, *both nervous and
happy, opens the door and gives a shout, which is almost
inaudible because of the loud sighing noise made by the engine
as it releases its steam.*

CAUSSAT (Louis Lefèbvre): Bruel!
BRUEL (Coco Golstein): Caussat!

CAUSSAT *helps another boy into his compartment. The
newcomer is dressed just like him (camera tilts slightly
downwards onto him), and is carrying the usual sailor's bag, as
well as the traditional food hamper. His name is* JULES BRUEL.
*Both for a lark and because they are in a hurry, the boys have
left the compartment door open (quick shot from the outside).
As the train leaves the station, a railway employee standing on
the platform quickly slams the door.*

 *

(and shouts)
The RAILWAY EMPLOYEE: Bloody kids!

*Back in the compartment, the two children are busy stashing
away their belongings and greeting each other. In the
background, the man continues to sleep in the seat opposite
them. Shot of the two of them, now sitting side by side, seen
slightly from above.*
*Apart from when they called out to each other cheerfully, the
boys have not exchanged a word so far. Still without speaking,
they begin to pull a variety of childish objects out of their*

* This text was in the script but was not filmed.

50

pocket, each odder than the previous one, with the obvious intention of impressing one another.

First, BRUEL *joins his hands and makes the knuckle of his thumb seem to detach itself from the rest of his hand; he then makes it seem to re-attach itself to the thumb (quick close-up).*

He then fishes a diabolo out of his pocket, tosses the ball up in the air several times and catches it. CAUSSAT *looks on admiringly, slaps him on the shoulder ... and stops him. It is his turn to take an amusing object out of his pocket: a miniature trumpet which he instantly puts on his lips.* BRUEL *looks on happily ... but* CAUSSAT *wants to improve his performance and removes the mouthpiece of the trumpet so as to place it in one of his nostrils, and attempts to play it with his nose (quick close-up).*

Immediately afterwards, BRUEL *takes out some balloons. He blows up first one, then a second, which* CAUSSAT *caresses as though it were a woman's breast .... They release the blown-up balloons, which rise to the ceiling of the compartment ...* CAUSSAT *then takes some feathers out of his pocket and leans over in his seat to hide what he is doing. He sticks a feather in his cap, another on his coat, another on his behind ... and then turns round.*

The camera is still during all of this time. As each object appears, the children express delight at their own finds, admiration for the gadgets produced by their pal, but also a touch of envy: each of them would like to outdo the other. After the feather, there is a pause in their game.

Have they run out of ideas or objects? Neither of them knew in advance that this splendid contest would take place. In fact, they are merely biding their time ... and both of them intend to take out that one object which the other could not possibly have thought of, given their age and their financial position. They look at each other as though both were thinking: 'Well! this time you'll be licked!' And simultaneously they pull out an enormous, identical cigar. They grin. Their first cigar! (the children are going to parody the adults).

Quick shot of the compartment door: the engine is spewing its smoke, which looks white through the window. The camera returns to the two children (still seen slightly from above). They

51

*light their cigars and pull on them, taking their first puffs (quick
shot of the compartment door and the engine smoke).*
*The two children, now seen from below, smoking their cigars
contentedly and pulling on them as though they were sucking at
the breast. The man is still asleep in his corner. The atmosphere
in the compartment is so misty by now that it takes on a
dreamlike quality. One of the balloons floats about in the
smoke ....*
*The boys are now feeling a bit queasy and they start looking
around. Another shot of the door of the smoke-laden
compartment, then close-up of the sleeping man, who is lying
on the seat (in the shot, to the left, the two children can be seen
from the back, staring at him).*

CAUSSAT: He's dead! ...

BRUEL, *worried, looks towards the compartment door. The
train is pulling in at a station.*

BRUEL: Let's get out of here!

*The train stops abruptly, shooting the sleeping man out of his
seat and onto the floor (sound of engines puffing and various
other station noises).*

A STATION PLATFORM — NIGHT

CAUSSAT *and* BRUEL, *seen from below, as they get out of the
train with their luggage onto a poorly-lit platform in a small
provincial station.*
*There are not many other travellers (group shot towards the
exit). Schoolboys in uniform, their sailor's bags on their
shoulders and carrying food hampers, are already standing in a
group near the exit, clustering round a man with a severe and
disagreeable face (close-up of his face, seen from below); he is
the school Superintendent, a man who, though he has somehow
managed to get the baccalauréat, has, through poverty of
intellect, ended up in this lowly position. His sole ambition
must limit itself to the hope of becoming Assistant Master some
day, after remaining in his present post for many a year to
come. His name is* MR PARRAIN, *known as 'Pète-Sec'.* *
* Pète-Sec = Dry Fart (*Translator's note*).

BRUEL, *off*: Look, Mr Pète-Sec! Won't be more fun this year than last.

CAUSSAT: Oh! ... you think not?

The camera returns to CAUSSAT, *in close-up, winking, then to* BRUEL, *also in close-up, who winks back at him. At that moment, a third schoolboy, dressed like them, comes up to them and winks too. His name is* JEAN COLIN. CAUSSAT *and* BRUEL *rush up to the boy they call 'Bean Kid'.* *

CAUSSAT and BRUEL: Hey! Bean Kid! ... we were on the train with a corpse!

COLIN (Gilbert Pruchon): A corpse! ....

CAUSSAT: A corpse! A corpse! ....

The group, seen from above.

PARRAIN: (Robert Le Flon): I say, Caussat, the holidays are over!

All the schoolboys cluster round the three friends to hear the story. Another boy arrives who is more distinguished-looking than the others. His name is RENÉ TABARD *and his appearance is extremely attractive. His expression is gentle, his manner somewhat too refined, his shyness and anxiety only too apparent. Though he is dressed like the other boys, he is much neater than they are (he wears a jacket, not a great-coat). He is wearing white gloves and is not carrying a sailor's bag or a hamper but a trim little suitcase. He hesitates as he goes up to Superintendent* PARRAIN *(the child is seen from above; we see the Superintendent from the back, in the foreground). Group shot: a pretty, elegant lady also goes up to Superintendent* PARRAIN *and takes the child by the shoulder.*

THE LADY: Excuse me, Sir, but René Tabard will not be coming until tomorrow.

Camera tilts down on the three of them (it is mainly THE LADY *we see. The Superintendent still has his back to the screen).*

THE LADY: He's feeling so sad this evening.

* Haricot Fils – so named because his mother is the school cook (*Translator's note*).

The Superintendent barely lifts his bowler hat to THE LADY *as she goes off with her son. Group shot.*

CAUSSAT: A corpse, I tell you ... a corpse ... the proof? ....
COLIN: The proof? ... there's the proof! ...

And indeed, we now see the gentleman who was in the compartment. He looks dazed, like someone who has just woken up, and is holding his luggage awry. He seems bewildered and at the same time delighted, half-smiling, as though looking for someone (he goes from left to right). Suddenly, he looks embarrassed and goes up to Superintendent PARRAIN *(alternate shots of the one and the other as they have the following dialogue).*

THE MAN (Jean Dasté): I'm the new Superintendent *(he raises his hat)* ... Superintendent Huguet.

Superintendent PARRAIN *replies with a very curt salute.*

PARRAIN: Ah! *(A pause, then he turns on the pupils)* Silence! Fall in line ... Get on, all of you!

The boys silently obey and disappear in the darkness, followed by PARRAIN ... *and by Superintendent* HUGUET *who still does not know how to handle all his luggage.*
Fade-out.

THE SCHOOL DORMITORY

Long shot of the dormitory.
Superintendent PARRAIN *is standing in the middle of the dormitory. The night watchman, standing at attention under the lamp, waits for the signal to turn down the light (group shot, seen slightly from above).*
All the children are in bed. At the four corners of the dormitory, CAUSSAT'S *bed,* BRUEL'S *bed,* COLIN'S *bed, and a fourth bed which is empty. No one moves and total silence reigns. Suddenly, a tall, thin man appears as if out of nowhere. No one has heard him come in. He wears a black coat, a soft felt hat with a broad brim and crêpe-soled shoes (he is the* HEAD SUPERINTENDENT*). He noiselessly crosses the entire length of*

54

*the dormitory, seeming to see nothing but in fact taking in
everything that is going on around him.*
*When he reaches the empty bed, he stops short but makes no
comment or gesture as* PARRAIN *explains:*

PARRAIN, *off*: René Tabard, absent. Will sleep at the hotel
tonight with his parents. Will arrive with the day-pupils
tomorrow.

The HEAD SUPERINTENDENT *leaves again noiselessly, and
vanishes (we hear a few notes on a flute).*
PARRAIN *says, just as the door closes on the* HEAD
SUPERINTENDENT:

PARRAIN: Goodnight, Sir.

(The HEAD SUPERINTENDENT *will reappear throughout the
film, always silently, when no one expects him, at the very
moment that the masters, children and servants would prefer
not to be seen by him.*
*He is a silent character, who never personally metes out
punishment, but who expects others to do so on his behalf. He
disappears just as he appears, silently. Each time he leaves, we
will hear the same little mocking tune on the flute.)*
When PARRAIN *gives the signal, the night watchman dims the
light and goes out. The room is in semi-darkness. The
Superintendent looks all round him at the beds, where the
children seem to be fast asleep.*
PARRAIN *then goes into his alcove, rubbing his hands. His bed
rests on a sort of platform in the middle of the dormitory, set
against one of the walls and curtained off by a semi-transparent
curtain, lit up by a candle from within. (*PARRAIN'S *shadow is
visible as he starts to undress.)*
As soon as PARRAIN *has gone into his alcove, we hear whispers
and stifled laughter. Someone barks like a dog; there is the
sound of a slap and louder laughter. Outwardly, nothing and
no one has moved.*

PARRAIN, *off*: Dupont, stand at the foot of my bed.

CAUSSAT, BRUEL *and* COLIN *(still seen from above) all get up
automatically, each of them believing that* PARRAIN *has called*

his name.

They have not heard which name PARRAIN *was calling out, but their conscience is never clear and they are accustomed to this punishment.*

All three therefore now stand in their slippers in front of the curtains round the Superintendent's bed, each one on a different side so that they are not aware of the presence of the other two.

CAUSSAT *coughs.*

BRUEL *coughs.*

COLIN *coughs.*

Guessing one another's presence now, they all cough again.

BRUEL *stretches out his arm to try and catch the pal who is standing on the other side of the curtained-off bed.* CAUSSAT *bites his finger.* BRUEL *cries out in pain.*

PARRAIN *sits up in bed and calls out (because we see the scene from above, we see him too, inside his alcove):*

PARRAIN: Who's there? Who's there?

CAUSSAT: Caussat, Sir.

BRUEL: Bruel, Sir.

COLIN: Colin, Sir.

Medium shot of two of the children standing in front of the curtains that shut off PARRAIN'S *bed.*

PARRAIN: Where's Dupont? ... I didn't call any of you three. Now you're there, you can stay there ... until 11 o'clock.

At that moment, we hear the clock strike nine and we see the entire dormitory from above as the night watchman re-enters, carrying a lantern with a strong beam. He walks past the three standing children without taking any notice of them. One of the boys, BRUEL, *suddenly doubles up and starts to wriggle in his nightshirt, his hands pressed to his stomach.*

BRUEL: Sir. (*Silence*) Sir, my stomach hurts ... Sir ....

CAUSSAT, *off*: Sir, can he be excused?

BRUEL: Sir ... my stomach hurts.

CAUSSAT, *off*: Sir, can he be excused?

COLIN, *off*: Sir, he's got a stomach-ache.

CAUSSET: Well, can he go or not? ... He's got a stomach-ache.

CAUSSET *and* COLIN *are now worried on their pal's behalf.*
They start to push BRUEL.

CAUSSAT: You go on out ... Don't you worry about that idiot.

The boy leaves, loudly slamming the dormitory door behind
him. The noise probably wakes PARRAIN *up.*

PARRAIN, *in a sleepy voice, off*: Caussat, Bruel and Colin, are
you there?
CAUSSAT *and* COLIN, *together*: Yes, Sir.
PARRAIN: Go to bed!

The two boys go to their beds ... just as BRUEL *comes in again.*
The camera pans along the beds of the sleeping children.
Medium close-up of one boy sitting up in bed, his head tilted
backward, brightly lit. The boy gets up and, sleepwalking,
starts to walk about in the dormitory. (General shot, seen from
above.)

A BOY: Go back to bed!
ANOTHER BOY: Be quiet! He'll die if you wake him. Quiet, I tell
you!
The sleepwalker returns to his bed and gets into it. Fade to the
same room at dawn.
The night watchman stolidly marches into the room and turns
out the night-light. We hear the roll of a drum out in the
courtyard. PARRAIN *instantly emerges from his alcove, fully*
dressed, and claps his hands as he goes from one bed to the
next.

PARRAIN: Up you get! Up you get! Quick now! Get up!

PARRAIN *pulls down the blankets on one bed ... and the child*
immediately pulls the blankets up again. PARRAIN *shakes one*
boy, pulls at the sheets of another, but all the kids stay in bed.

PARRAIN: Well, what is it? ... Are you deaf?
ONE BOY, *off*: Ah ... stop bothering me. Leave me alone!

The HEAD SUPERINTENDENT *suddenly appears and walks*
down the aisle in silence, as he always does. As he passes in
front of each bed, the boy who occupies that bed springs up and
stands to attention. By the time the HEAD SUPERINTENDENT

has crossed the dormitory and left by the door at the far end, everybody is up.
The moment he leaves, however, BRUEL, COLIN *and* CAUSSAT *get back into their beds (medium close-up of each of them).*
Between two beds, a younger boy rushes over to a chamber-pot and kneels in front of it (shot from the back). Quick shot of the door being reopened softly: the HEAD SUPERINTENDENT *reappears and looks around.*

PARRAIN, *off*: Bruel, Caussat, Colin, nought for conduct. You'll be kept in on Sunday.

Quick shot of CAUSSAT *getting up again, furious.*

CAUSSAT: Well! ... I can see nothing's changed!
PARRAIN, *off*: Now Bruel, are you late again?

The HEAD SUPERINTENDENT *disappears, closing the door behind him.*

 *

The boarders are washing at the basin which stands in the middle of the dormitory. They are all in their shirt-sleeves except for one who has taken off his vest to wash better and is bare to the waist. The HEAD SUPERINTENDENT *appears from nowhere and notices the bare-chested boy.* PARRAIN *rushes up to the culprit with a blanket, screaming:*

PARRAIN: Aren't you ashamed of yourself, you devil!

The HEAD SUPERINTENDENT *disappears again.*
A brief montage sequence follows which shows what life at the school is like. The sequence, which is punctuated by the sound of hands clapping, of drums rolling and of adults calling out 'Kept in on Sunday' tends to demonstrate how the children's spontaneity is constantly being repressed.
This very rapid sequence is treated in a spirit of comedy rather than tragedy, and will make a welcome break for the spectator as it is not chronological, unlike the events that precede and follow it.

* These scenes were not shot but were in Vigo's original script.

Examples: the children walk down the stairs, two by two (to the sound of rolling drums).

The schoolyard: the children rush out into the schoolyard (clapping of hands).

The image freezes for a few seconds on the screen so that the children who were running about and playing seem to be caught off balance, in odd, awkward positions; their freedom of movement is always being curtailed (sound of hand-clapping).

In the dining-hall: a boy is drinking coffee. He suddenly bursts out laughing and spurts coffee all over his neighbour (sound of drums rolling).

A VOICE, *off*: Kept in on Sunday!

The children, as if on drill.

The children are marching towards camera. They start to sing. We hear their song, then the sound stops on a high note and holds there for a few seconds.

All the children's mouths are open.

The scene in which the children march singing towards the camera, in reverse motion.

The pupils seem to be sucked back by some strong force – a door shuts on them (sound of clapping hands).

VOICE, *off*: Kept in on Sunday!

End of this brief sequence, which is a condensed version of life at the school.

━━━━━━━━━━━━━━━━━━━━

Jean Vigo replaced this sequence, which was not filmed, with another that takes place in the dormitory. The children are dressed and are standing by their beds. PARRAIN *claps his hands; they form a line and walk out of the room, none of them misbehaving, all of them a bit sleepy.*

PARRAIN, *off*: Get a move on over there ... Quickly ... I say, do you want to get nought for conduct?

Fade-out in black on an insert, on which the following words are written:

THE CHILDREN HATCH A PLOT

THE SCHOOL YARD

Medium close-up of three children, seen from above. They are wearing black school smocks and are squatting on the ground, solemnly hatching their plot.

CAUSSAT: My friends, here's the plan. Our plan is ready. We're kept in every Sunday ... we must run away.
BRUEL: Through the roof?
COLIN: What about the ammunition?
BRUEL: Caussat has found out where the food's kept.

Camera pans down in a long shot of the school yard. Then a close-up of little Tabard, who stands some distance away from the others, leaning against a tree.

CAUSSAT: Why is Tabard looking at us?
COLIN, *off*: He's a sneak. Let's go and beat him up.

Shot of the new Superintendent, HUGUET, *wearing a bowler hat and carrying a cane, as he walks up and down the yard. He is obviously bored and seems to want to join in the boys' games. Without paying any attention to the trio, he walks towards them. Medium close-up of his legs, very close to the three children.*

CAUSSAT: Watch it! The junior master!
COLIN, *off*: Oh! ... Huguet? He's all right!

The three boys get up. One of them jumps onto the other's back while the third follows behind. They move off, and head towards a building; still very conspiratorial, they look suspiciously both to the left and the right before they enter one of the classrooms.
We return to HUGUET. *The camera pans to follow him as he amuses himself by walking backwards in the schoolyard until he reaches the toilets. Inside adjoining toilets, two boys are taking puffs from the same cigarette in secret, handing it backward and forward to each other.* HUGUET *does not notice them and is slouching dreamily when, all of a sudden, a ball*

lands on him. *He grabs it and starts to run, followed by a dozen kids. They stop pursuing him when they catch sight of the* HEAD SUPERINTENDENT, *but* HUGUET *throws them the ball and the children run after it.* HUGUET *raises his hat to the* HEAD SUPERINTENDENT *and moves towards the other side of the courtyard. The camera tracks after* HUGUET, *whose walk and mannerisms increasingly resemble those of Charlie Chaplin. The children watch him, following him and hiding when he turns round.*

(Little by little, the whole scene turns into a parody of the classic scene in Easy Street, *a sort of cinematic homage to Chaplin, an equivalent to quoting a well-known passage by a famous writer in a literary work.* HUGUET *will appear throughout the film as a dreamer but also as someone full of vitality, who feels closer to* CAUSSAT, BRUEL *and* COLIN *than to the school authorities which he is meant to represent.)*

Close-up in profile of the HEAD SUPERINTENDENT. *The camera pans down to his feet. With mincing steps, he heads for the classroom where the three boys are hiding.*

THE CLASSROOM

Quick medium close-up of the classroom, seen from above. CAUSSAT *is drawing a skull and cross bones on a black piece of cloth. The 'flag' is soon hidden away.*

CAUSSAT: And so, on the great day, we plant the flag ....
BRUEL, *off*: What about the ammunition?
COLIN, *off*: The lamp-post!*

SCHOOL COURTYARD

The camera returns to the HEAD SUPERINTENDENT *who is about to creep into the classroom just as the three children leap out of the window and run off to join their schoolfellows.*

THE CLASSROOM

Stealthily, with his springy dancer's step, the HEAD

* Lamp-post = 'Bec de gaz', the name the children give the Head Superintendent (*Translator's note*).

SUPERINTENDENT *closes the door behind him and inspects the classroom. He then goes and searches through a few school desks (camera pans after him in long shot). He notices a small parcel which he grabs and opens: it contains some chocolate, which he eats immediately. He takes one or two more things out of the desk, goes to the centre of the classroom, looks inside a satchel and finds a letter in it, which he pockets hastily.*

THE SCHOOLYARD

A group of boys stand round the toilets, knocking on the only door which shuts properly. The new junior master comes out of the toilet and races off with a runner's sprint, chased by the children.
Quick shot of a boy roughly pulling the door of the toilets open, hoping to surprise one of his pals whom he thinks is having a secret smoke inside there.

⌐‾‾‾‾‾‾‾‾‾‾‾‾‾⌐   *

A succession of shots of different groups of children.
JULES BRUEL *and* RENÉ TABARD *are very close friends and seem to be quite demonstrative with one another. There is nothing ambivalent about their relationship, however, and their feelings for each other are completely innocent. The school authorities are nevertheless keeping a watchful eye on the two boys.*
TABARD *admires* BRUEL, CAUSSAT *and* COLIN, *but he is not allowed to conspire with them, for* CAUSSAT *and* COLIN *do not want to include him.*

CAUSSAT: Where will we go?

COLIN *points to a skylight close to the roof.* BRUEL *moves closer.*

BRUEL: When?
CAUSSAT: When we decide to.
COLIN: When will we raise our flag up there?
BRUEL: What about the supplies?
CAUSSAT: The cakes for the school fête on the 15th.

* These scenes were never shot.

62

At the far end of the courtyard, we see a delivery-boy whom HUGUET *sends to* MRS COLIN, *the 'Bean Lady' who is* COLIN'S *mother. Several brief references to the school fête will be made in the course of the film. The final scenes of the film will take place during this fête.*

COLIN: The stores in the kitchen, too. I'll steal the keys from my mother.
BRUEL: Oh! It'll be ....
COLIN, *sadly:* Yes, beans again.
CAUSSAT, *affectionately:* Poor old Bean Kid!

At that moment, a boy comes over to them and says:

THE BOY: Bean Kid, Ma Bean wants to speak to you.

> COLIN *gets up to go and look for his mother, the fat school cook with the blue apron. As he walks past the boy who came to fetch him, he tries to kick him on the backside.*
> *From afar, the* HEAD SUPERINTENDENT *seems to be wondering what* CAUSSAT *is up to. The child is instantly terrified that his written plan will be discovered.*
> *Without seeming to,* HUGUET *comes to his rescue by stopping in front of him and thus hiding the boy with his body from the* HEAD SUPERINTENDENT'S *gaze; this gives* CAUSSAT *time to hide the plan inside his pocket.*
> CAUSSAT *then tries to appear innocent and rushes over to a ball which is rolling in his direction. He gives it a kick ... and breaks a window (sound of broken glass). The* HEAD SUPERINTENDENT *instantly reappears.* CAUSSAT *goes up to him obediently to face the music ... . He will be kept in yet another Sunday.*

CAUSSAT: Kept in on Sunday.

> *The* HEAD SUPERINTENDENT *disappears.*
> CAUSSAT *returns to the yard just as the ball comes flying at him, hits him on the head and bounces from his skull to a window further up (more sound of breaking glass).*
> *The* HEAD SUPERINTENDENT *reappears and there is a repeat of the scene we have just witnessed.* CAUSSAT *once again gives a helpless shrug and walks over to the* HEAD SUPERINTENDENT.

CAUSSAT: Two Sundays.

CAUSSAT *is about to return to the yard, but this time he is on the lookout for any stray balls. Once again, the* HEAD SUPERINTENDENT *vanishes into his office.*

The ball is thrown at CAUSSAT *again. He ducks to avoid it and it sails past him in the direction of the* HEAD SUPERINTENDENT'S *office.*

The HEAD SUPERINTENDENT *hastily closes his office door, which has a glass panel. The ball breaks the glass pane on which the words 'Head Superintendent' are written (more sound of breaking glass).*

The HEAD SUPERINTENDENT *reappears and* CAUSSAT *in utter despair, goes up to him to be punished yet another time (repeat of the same scene).*

The HEAD SUPERINTENDENT *disappears once more.*

Furious, CAUSSAT *hurls himself on the ball and now aims it at every window in sight; but this time everything seems to be conspiring to prevent him from breaking any more windows. In a rage,* CAUSSAT *aims the ball at the* HEAD SUPERINTENDENT *who is coming out of his office.*

At that instant, HUGUET *appears, on his way to the classroom. Without seeming to, always giving the impression of being a bit vague and 'out of it', he forces the* HEAD SUPERINTENDENT *to move slightly to one side, so that the ball flies past his head. He freezes in his tracks to wait for the sound of broken glass, but* HUGUET *raises his hat to the* HEAD SUPERINTENDENT *and manages to catch the ball in it.*

HUGUET *then places his hat, still containing the ball, onto his head again. It makes the top of his head look disproportionately high as he enters the classroom.*

⎣▬▬▬▬▬▬▬▬▬▬▬⎦

The children who have watched the scene are delighted. They all run into the classroom after HUGUET.

The school break is over. Just as the children reach the door of the classroom, the drum is heard rolling.

INSIDE THE CLASSROOM

HUGUET *is sitting at his desk. As always, he looks a bit weary each time he finds himself in a position of having to give orders. The children come into the classroom, crestfallen.* HUGUET *shrugs his shoulders.*

HUGUET: Go to your seats. Come along now .... To your seats!

Long shot of the classroom, which is like any other classroom: the master's desk on a raised platform, the pupils' desks, the lockers along the walls ... those very lockers which the HEAD SUPERINTENDENT *searched earlier on. A window set in the wall makes it possible to see everything going on in the classroom from outside.*
CAUSSAT *grabs the ball, which is lying on the floor, and holds it at arm's length, getting ready to hurl it at one of his pals.*
The HEAD SUPERINTENDENT *appears at the window.*
CAUSSAT *blows on the ball, which vanishes (shot from above).*
The HEAD SUPERINTENDENT *moves away from the window.*
CAUSSAT *pretends to be a great conjurer and, to his friends' delight, makes the ball reappear at the tip of his fingers. He then goes and puts the ball in his locker and cries out:*

CAUSSAT: Colin's taken my chocolate!

The HEAD SUPERINTENDENT *reappears at the window as* COLIN *makes a gesture of the head towards the window.*

COLIN: He's been searching.
CAUSSAT: Aha! So he's been searching, has he? Wait! Give me my pot of glue.

The HEAD SUPERINTENDENT *moves away from the window.* CAUSSAT *moves about the classroom, asking everybody to lend him a pot of glue (the camera tracks forward then pans towards the lockers).*

CAUSSAT: Your glue ... Your pot of glue.

Each boy hands over his glue and CAUSSAT *carefully and deliberately empties each pot behind the books inside the lockers.*

The camera suddenly returns to HUGUET, *who seems to take a keen interest in what the boys are doing. He steps down from the platform on which his desk stands (quick close-up of* CAUSSAT'S *hands pouring out the glue). One boy is walking on his hands.* HUGUET *looks at him, helps him to straighten his spine and holds up his feet. In the end,* HUGUET *gives a personal demonstration of his skills: after taking off his jacket, he too starts walking about on his hands. He then returns to his desk, still walking on his hands, manages to climb in this fashion first onto the platform, then onto his chair and finally, onto the desk itself. The children are highly impressed.*

HUGUET: Hand me the paper, over there in the drawer ... some ink ... now hand me the pen ... there!

In his acrobatic posture, he draws a caricature of the HEAD SUPERINTENDENT.

HUGUET: Now, look!

The HEAD SUPERINTENDENT *appears at the door, after a quick shot of him outside in the courtyard, going into the classroom.*
The classroom is an odd sight for the HEAD SUPERINTENDENT: *the pupils are smoking and ostentatiously reading newspapers; a few of them are playing at marbles; others deal cards. Others are fighting. There is a great concentration of boys in the centre of the room. One child is fast asleep, snoring.* CAUSSAT, COLIN *and* BRUEL *are studying their plan.* HUGUET *immediately returns to his normal position and stands next to his desk.*
The HEAD SUPERINTENDENT *and* HUGUET *look at the scene; the former seems to be saying: 'Yes, yes, I see: of course. So what?' (quick shot of him, then group shot once more). The* HEAD SUPERINTENDENT *now climbs up onto the platform and looks (the camera tilts down) at the caricature of himself which is lying on* HUGUET'S *desk. At that moment the drawing comes to life: the figure changes and no longer looks like the* HEAD SUPERINTENDENT *but like a woman, then like Napoleon. (End of the cartoon sequence.)*
The HEAD SUPERINTENDENT *looks in the direction of the door.* PARRAIN *is just coming in to replace* HUGUET.

HUGUET: Go to your seats.

HUGUET, *who seemed to be paying no attention to what had been going on in the classroom, had nonetheless taken in everything. Before leaving, he goes over to the desk where* CAUSSAT, BRUEL *and* COLIN *are sitting together, trying to conceal their written plan.*

HUGUET: Give me that.

He grabs the bit of paper, tears it in two and puts the pieces in his pocket. He then leaves the room. (We will understand later that HUGUET *was doing this only to help* CAUSSAT, BRUEL *and* COLIN, *whose plan was about to be confiscated by the* HEAD SUPERINTENDENT.*)*
The HEAD SUPERINTENDENT *leaves the classroom.*
PARRAIN *climbs onto the platform. All the pupils quickly go back to their desks (shot of* PARRAIN, *seen from above, sitting at his desk).*
PARRAIN *takes a pen out of his pocket and starts writing down in his notebook the various punishments that have been given to the boys.*
Fade-out in black.

THE SCHOOL YARD

The children are in the yard, standing in rank as they wait to go on an outing. In the background, we see HUGUET. *The* HEAD SUPERINTENDENT *comes into shot and* HUGUET *greets him. He returns* HUGUET'S *greeting.*
The HEAD SUPERINTENDENT *then inspects the ranks of boys … , and rushes to separate* TABARD *and* BRUEL, *whom he does not want to see side by side. He parts them, straightens the cap of one boy and finishes his inspection. Suddenly, he starts to wriggle with emotion.*

PARRAIN: Here comes the Headmaster!

The HEAD SUPERINTENDENT *instantly starts to bow so low that his pince-nez drops to the ground (he quickly picks it up).* *

* In his script, Vigo intended to show the Head Superintendent trying once again to steal from the pupils, before this scene took place. He would not have dropped his pince-nez in that case, but would have been trying desperately to wipe glue off his hands, his hat and his handkerchief.

He then raises his hat, as do PARRAIN, HUGUET *and all the children.*
A midget appears from the left, wearing a frock-coat and a bowler hat. He has a long, brown beard. He greets everyone.

PARRAIN: Sir....

The HEADMASTER *goes up to the children (he is much shorter than them), seems to find everything in order and nods approvingly at* PARRAIN.

PARRAIN, *to* HUGUET *and to the children:* We go now, gentlemen.

The group sets off, led by HUGUET. *As the* HEADMASTER *starts walking back towards the school buildings, he says:*

HEADMASTER: Head Superintendent, will you please come to my office?

The HEAD SUPERINTENDENT, *as full of deference as ever, follows the little man.*

A CITY STREET

The schoolboys walk along the pavement in rows of two, according to height, wearing their uniform. They are singing.
HUGUET *walks with them, but in the middle of the street, a dreamy look on his face. (The camera tracks back so that the boys are walking towards camera. The camera then tracks forward and we now see the children from the back.) During the second tracking shot we see* TABARD *slipping out of his place in the ranks to join* BRUEL.
Fade-out.

THE HEADMASTER'S OFFICE

Seen from behind, the HEADMASTER *comes in and goes over to the fireplace. The* HEAD SUPERINTENDENT *follows him and stops in the centre of the room.*
Medium close-up of the HEADMASTER *next to the fireplace. He takes his hat off and tries to slip it onto the mantlepiece, which he has some difficulty in reaching. He then lifts a large glass*

cloche and slips his hat underneath it, on his tiptoes throughout.[*] *Having accomplished this task, he goes to his desk with a satisfied expression. Quick shot of the* HEADMASTER *turning to look at himself in the large mirror over the mantlepiece. We can see the* HEAD SUPERINTENDENT *reflected in it, full-length. The* HEADMASTER *smoothes back his hair with his hand, and the* HEAD SUPERINTENDENT *decides to do the same.*

HEADMASTER: Please be seated.

The camera is placed near the ground, as though we were seeing the scene from the HEADMASTER'S *height. Shot of the* HEAD SUPERINTENDENT'S *legs from this angle, as he takes a seat opposite the desk.*
The camera returns to the HEADMASTER *behind his desk. Before climbing onto his chair, he smoothes his beard.*
Now that he is seated, we can see that his feet, which do not reach the ground, are inside a fleecy foot-cover, to protect them from the cold. (Shot of the two men, seen from above, favouring the HEADMASTER.)

HEADMASTER: Our fête, dear Mr Sant – it's your little festivity, isn't it? – will take place soon .... But whatever happens, no problems, no incidents!

A CITY STREET

Quick shot of the children on their walk. HUGUET *looks dreamier than ever (the camera tracks forward; we see the characters from the back). The boys, who know their way by heart, turn left at a given point.* HUGUET, *whose attention has been caught by a piece of paper which he takes out of his pocket and throws away, walks straight on, loudly whistling the tune which the boys are singing. The camera follows him for a moment as he walks on, alone. Since the beginning of this scene, we have heard the* HEADMASTER, *off, pursuing his conversation with the* HEAD SUPERINTENDENT.

HEADMASTER: By the way, what about Bruel, Caussat and

[*] The two following gags were not in the script. Vigo must have improvised them during shooting.

69

Colin? As for Monsieur Huguet, whom I believed to be so respectable ....

THE HEADMASTER'S OFFICE

Same camera position, tilting down, but favouring the HEAD SUPERINTENDENT *rather than the* HEADMASTER.

HEADMASTER: ... What you tell me about him worries me .... To conclude, Mr Sant ..., according to you, Sir ... Tabard and Bruel are behaving like little children, like ragamuffins ... Not serious, not serious at all ....

CITY STREETS

Quick shots of the children, seen from above, as they race about the city, happy to be on their own. Shot of HUGUET *coming out of a tobacconist's shop.* PARRAIN *sees him and stares in astonishment. The young man greets him blithely and goes off. Quick shot of* HUGUET, *walking in a dream. The camera tracks backwards in a close-up of* HUGUET *looking up in the air, raising his hat to salute an imaginary muse.*
Long shot of the children, seen from far above, as they start looking for HUGUET *after much running to their hearts' content. They want to find* HUGUET *as much for his sake as for their own.*

⌐‾‾‾‾‾‾‾‾‾‾‾‾‾‾‾‾‾‾‾‾¬ *

The boys rush over to a sweet cart, where an enormously fat lady sells barley sugar, oranges, etc. The SWEET LADY *is sitting on a little bench behind her cart, which is shaded by a parasol. The boys start to bait her and try to steal her goods (a few of them try to make her fall off her seat, and to catch a glimpse of her plump calves in the process. Others tie the tassels of the parasol to the half-belt of their pals' coats.)*
The outraged SWEET LADY *lunges at the boys, but they instantly start flashing small mirrors at her, blinding her with sun-spots, preventing her from catching them.*
CAUSSAT, BRUEL *and* COLIN *suddenly appear, carrying an*

---

* This scene was not shot.

*enormous looking-glass which lights up the fat lady from head to foot. H*UGUET *comes out of the tobacconist's at that moment. He can see her silhouette through her dress as clearly as if the cloth were transparent.*

*The boys have finally met up with H*UGUET *again, and are now following him. The young man does not seem to notice their presence.*
*Suddenly, a smartly-dressed young woman comes out of a house and crosses H*UGUET'S *path. H*UGUET *immediately starts to follow her, quickening his step to keep up with her. The boys follow behind him. The pretty young woman, embarrassed, walks on even faster. H*UGUET *and all the children hurry after her. Perhaps intrigued, she turns to look at H*UGUET, *who raises his hat high in the air to her. All the boys follow his example and raise their caps. She walks on, still followed by H*UGUET *and the children.*
The master and the boys are now literally running in pursuit of the young woman. As they chase her through the city streets, some of the kids trip and fall down.
*The young woman disappears round a corner. H*UGUET *hesitates for a second and then continues the chase.*
*Medium close-up of a black skirt disappearing round another street corner. H*UGUET *catches sight of the skirt and rushes after it. It's a mistake. H*UGUET *finds himself nose to nose with a Priest, who looks up at him furiously, then starts reading his breviary. H*UGUET *disappears. Shot of the Priest trotting off in another direction.*
Fade-out.

THE HEADMASTER'S OFFICE

*Same shot of the H*EADMASTER *and the H*EAD SUPERINTENDENT *talking as before. (The shot favours the H*EADMASTER.)

HEADMASTER: … And will you consider our responsibility from the moral point of view?

Fade-out in black.

71

CITY STREETS

                 *

HUGUET *goes into a street urinal. The boys wait, in rows of two. (In the course of this excursion, we will have seen* CAUSSAT, BRUEL *and* COLIN *wanting to help out* HUGUET, *just as the master comes to their rescue at the school. Throughout the film, the boys and the master will try to come to each other's aid, though these attempts will always remain unspoken.)*
COLIN, BRUEL *and* CAUSSAT *think up another stratagem. All three take off their greatcoats and start using them like toreadors use their capes.* HUGUET *finally snaps out of his dream state and, allowing himself to be carried away by their game, hurls himself on their coats like a bull. For a moment, they play at bullfighting.*
It starts raining and night falls.
The boys run back to their school, hugging the wall.

THE SCHOOL YARD – NIGHT

Close to the main entrance of the school, the HEADMASTER *and the* HEAD SUPERINTENDENT *are waiting under an umbrella, which the* HEADMASTER *holds high above their heads (camera pans down slightly onto them).*
Quick shot of HUGUET *hastily entering the school yard and, as he goes past the two men, raising his hat to them both without slowing down.*

HEADMASTER: Monsieur Huguet comes back all by himself? … What an excursion!… It is intolerable!….

Shot of the school gate. Two children slip into the school yard … then another two. The taller of these is holding the skirt of his greatcoat over the head of the smaller one. The camera returns to the HEADMASTER *and the* HEAD SUPERINTENDENT, *seen from below.*

* This scene was not shot.

HEADMASTER: There we go again! The two of them together. Their friendship is becoming excessive. (*A pause.*) Mr Sant, you are right ... They must be watched.

The HEADMASTER *and the* HEAD SUPERINTENDENT *look at one another. To them, it is quite obvious that* BRUEL *and* TABARD *are different from the others.*

 *

DORMITORY – NIGHT

The light is soft and bright. We see what the dormitory is like in the evening. One child is perched on his night-table, and is reading by the night-lamp. Another is reading, buried under his blankets, lighting his book with a torch.
COLIN *and* CAUSSAT *have found their plan under their eiderdown carefully stuck together and put there by* HUGUET. *The two boys discuss 'D-Day' and say:*

CAUSSAT: Bruel is a nuisance, always telling us about his Tabard.
COLIN: His Tabard will end up by betraying us.

They go over to BRUEL'S *bed from time to time. Shot of* TABARD *who is sitting on* BRUEL'S *bed.*

TABARD, *to Bruel*: Do you think Caussat and Colin will accept me?

The other children are watching BRUEL *and* TABARD.
We see PARRAIN'S *shadow through the curtains of the alcove, which is lit up from within by a candle. He is giving himself an injection.*
The children are now asleep.
The children are dreaming aloud.
The sleepwalker is sleepwalking.
CAUSSAT *and* COLIN *go over to* BRUEL'S *bed. According to them, another boy intends to betray them. They punch the sneak in the stomach.* TABARD, *still sitting on* BRUEL'S *bed, looks on and recalls that he too is unfairly suspected by* CAUSSAT *and* COLIN.
* This scene was not shot.

Back in his bed, BRUEL *wants to reassure* TABARD. *Before bidding him goodnight, he pulls on the piece of chewing-gum in his mouth and sticks the end bit on the tip of* TABARD'S *nose. Their lips and nose more or less stuck to each other, they exchange a friendly look.*
The HEAD SUPERINTENDENT *comes upon them at that moment. (We hear a few notes on the flute.)*

THE HEADMASTER'S OFFICE

Shot of the HEADMASTER *sitting at his desk, seen from above. Before his desk,* TABARD *is standing shyly, listening to a speech which he cannot understand and growing more embarrassed every minute.*

HEADMASTER: My little fellow ... I'm almost like a father to you .... At your age, there are things, are there not? ... which ... In a word, Bruel is older than you .... *(Close-up of Tabard as the headmaster continues, off)* ... your nature, your sensitivity, his ... You understand?

TABARD *no longer knows what is allowed and what is not. After all the surreptitious spying on him and* BRUEL *at the school, the* HEADMASTER'S *ambiguous words make him feel that something shameful has been going on, though he is not sure what it was supposed to be. He will no longer dare to react like an uninhibited child. Any physical contact is going to be intolerable to him from now on, every word fraught with innuendo. The situation is going to make him so nervous that the outburst we shall soon witness will be the logical outcome of his inner tension.*

HEADMASTER: ... You know ... neurotics ... psychopaths .... Heaven only knows!

As he pronouces these final words, the HEADMASTER *gets up, raising his arms to Heaven, his eyes popping out of his head (the camera tilts down on him).*
Fade-out in black.

THE CLASSROOM

TABARD *comes into the classroom, under the watchful eye of* PARRAIN. *He goes and sits at a desk a long way away from* BRUEL, *who does not understand and calls out to him in a whisper:*

BRUEL: Come over here, next to me …. Come on!

The door flies open and a voice calls out:

THE VOICE: Colin, Caussat, to the parlour.

(On Sunday, which is theoretically the day when the boys are allowed out, BRUEL *stays at the school,* CAUSSAT *visits friends of his family, and* COLIN *remains with his mother in the school kitchen.)*
The two boys get up when their name is called out. The tallest of the two, CAUSSAT, *is dressed to go out. He crosses the room, followed by* COLIN. *They both pause before the* SUPERINTENDENT'S *desk and bow to him in an exaggerated, grandiloquent fashion.*

PARRAIN: I say! Do you want to be kept in again?

THE SCHOOL YARD

CAUSSAT *and* COLIN *are walking along a wooden picket fence, towards camera. They walk stiffly, with great dignity, then stop and stand face to face (medium shot). They bow formally to each other and* CAUSSAT *bursts out laughing.*

COLIN: That's a proper Sunday bow. I have to stay here with my ma … in the kitchen … while you go and visit your chicks.

*(*CAUSSAT *laughs even louder.)*

Fade-out in black, then insert:–

'SUNDAY: CAUSSAT AT THE HOUSE OF FRIENDS.'

THE DINING-ROOM AT THE FRIENDS' HOUSE

It is a Rococo-style dining-room, with a Henry the Second table

75

next to an upright piano. The family friend (whom we never see) is reading his newspaper. CAUSSAT *is sitting very quietly in the background; he is blindfolded. A charming little girl is squatting on the piano, preparing a surprise for* CAUSSAT. *She will slip a goldfish bowl on a string just in front of the blindfolded boy and, when she has finished doing this, she will return to her place next to him and remove his blindfold.* CAUSSAT'S *expression is one of wonder and delight.* *.
Fade-out, then insert: –

'... AND COLIN WITH MA BEAN, HIS MOTHER'

THE SCHOOL KITCHEN

Shot of young COLIN *sitting on a bench in the kitchen. The camera tracks back to reveal a long shot of the kitchen with, in the foreground to the right, the cooking stove on which several saucepans and stewpots are simmering.* COLIN'S *mother appears and goes over to the stove. She lifts the lid off one of the stewpots.*
In the background, COLIN *looks out of the skylight.*

OUTSIDE THE KITCHEN

In the school yard, squatting close to the kitchen skylight which gives onto the playground, BRUEL *is signalling to* COLIN, *who is inside.*
The camera pans across to TABARD, *who comes closer.*

BRUEL: Tabard, come on over here ....

Saying these words, BRUEL *shows the skylight to* TABARD, *who bends over to look at* COLIN.

THE KITCHEN

The mother is still at her stove, the son on his bench, playing with a ball. The mother glances at her son to see if he is being good, then looks away again. He tosses the ball out of the

---

* Jean Vigo stressed in the script: 'This very pure scene reveals Caussat to be a very sensitive, delicate boy'.

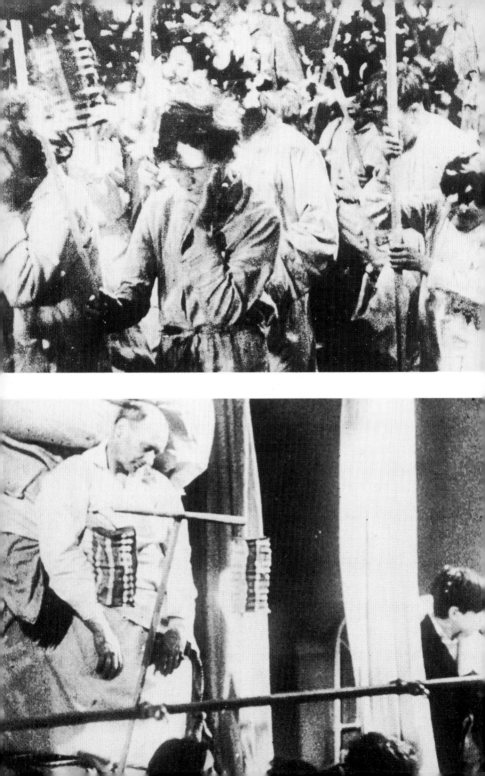

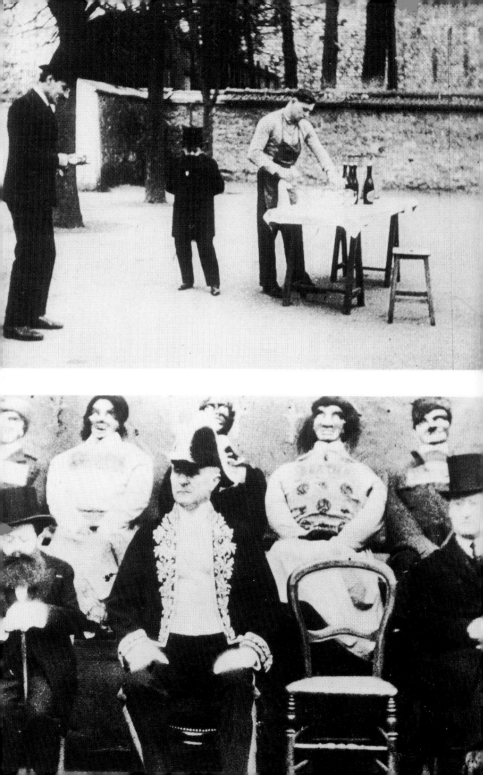

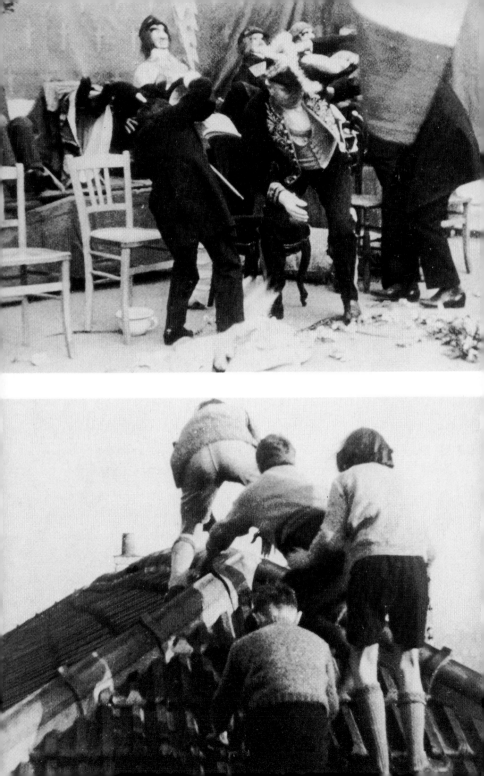

skylight on purpose, then rushes out of the kitchen to go and fetch the ball.

THE SCHOOL YARD

COLIN *comes running over to his pals, who are still next to the skylight.*

BRUEL, *off:* Give Tabard the chocolate, Colin.

COLIN *runs over to* TABARD, *who is getting up from his squatting position near the skylight. He looks at* TABARD *suspiciously. Shot of the three children, seen slightly from above. Then close-up of* COLIN, *hesitating.*

BRUEL, *off:* Look, I promise you he's not a sneak. He's a pal. Caussat's wrong to keep him out of the plot *(close-up of* BRUEL*).* I'm telling you, look, I'm telling you … *(close-up of* TABARD, *smiling)…* besides, he's got a hiding-place, you'll see, he'll help us. *(Close-up of* COLIN, *won over and smiling too.)* He doesn't like the teachers. I swear he doesn't like them.

Close-up of COLIN'S *hands pulling a chocolate bar out of his pocket.*
He gives it to TABARD.
Fade-out.

THE KITCHEN

Same long shot of the kitchen as in the previous scenes. COLIN'S *mother is busy cooking. In the background, we see the* HEAD SUPERINTENDENT *coming down the stairs into the kitchen and walking over to the stove.*

MA BEAN (*Mme Emile*): Ah! Mr Superintendent!

The HEAD SUPERINTENDENT *lifts the lid off one of the stewpots and sniffs the odour.*

MA BEAN: Yes, beans, always beans. (*The* HEAD SUPERINTENDENT *shrugs*) …. Yet I can't always be serving beans to those children.

The HEAD SUPERINTENDENT *ignores her words and leaves the kitchen. The cook raises her arms to heaven in a gesture of helplessness.*

A few seconds go by: COLIN'S *mother is still busy at the stove. Her son comes in, walks over to the stove, and as his mother is lifting a pot lid he looks in to see what is cooking.*

COLIN: Oh! ma! ... not beans again!

The cook slaps her son. He hurls the ball down to protect his face with his hands and runs off. The ball bounces off the ground and lands in the stewpot. The mother, even more furious, fishes it out and throws it at the child, who catches it just as he is leaving the room.

THE DINING-HALL

The dining-hall with its rows of tables is seen from above. The children arrive in rows and sit down to eat. PARRAIN *looks on nonchalantly. As soon as the boys are seated, there is a terrible din.*

⌐￣￣￣￣￣￣￣￣￣⌐   *

CAUSSAT *who has been ordered to keep silent by* PARRAIN *mimes his afternoon visit for the benefit of his pals.*

We have already seen the scene that took place between CAUSSAT *and the sweet little girl on Sunday afternoon. Nothing happened except for the most innocent of childish games, so that we are not taken in when we see* CAUSSAT, *that evening, miming a completely different version of the event in order to impress his friends.*

CAUSSAT *becomes over-enthusiastic and his pals begin to be sceptical. One of them says:*

BOY: It ain't true!

CAUSSAT *senses that he is about to forfeit his schoolfellows' trust. He catches hold of a piece of hemp rope which is hanging out of the pocket of a boy sitting behind him at another table. He quickly shreds the piece of rope behind his back and produces the bit of tow, declaring:*

CAUSSAT: Well, what about this? Is it true or not?

* These scenes were not shot.

CAUSSAT'S *pals look down admiringly, saying:*

BOYS: Hair! .... Her hair! .... Give me some of it!

CAUSSAT *triumphantly places the pieces of shredded rope inside his wallet.*

⌐————————————————————⌐

The dishes arrive (different shots of the dining hall, mainly seen from above).
There is pandemonium when the boys see that it is beans again.
COLIN *shouts as loud as the rest of them (he remembers the slap he received). The noise is deafening with shouts and the sound of crockery.*

THE CHILDREN, *shouting:* Boo to Ma Bean! (*repeated several times*) Boo! Yah! .... Boo!

By now, COLIN *is close to tears for he is thinking: 'Ma Bean! It's my mother, after all, who prepared those beans'. (Close-up* COLIN *as he hangs his head).*

PARRAIN,*off*: Come now!

CAUSSAT *and* BRUEL *immediately grasp* COLIN'S *distress and try to stop the others from shouting.*

CAUSSAT: Enough! Be quiet!

┌————————————————————┐ *

The HEAD SUPERINTENDENT *appears. Calm has been restored well before he enters the room.*

└————————————————————┘

THE CHEMISTRY CLASSROOM

The classroom is empty, seen slightly from above. Only CAUSSAT *and* COLIN *are present, talking, close to the heater.*†

---

* This scene was not shot.
† In his script, Vigo had planned a scene before the chemistry lesson, in which the children would be discussing Tabard. In his book on Vigo, P.E. Salès Gomès claims that the scene was shot but that Vigo cut it because he felt the sequence which was to come would have more dramatic intensity if it were not preceded by the gag about a smoke-filled stovepipe.

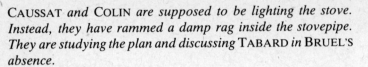
*

CAUSSAT and COLIN are supposed to be lighting the stove. Instead, they have rammed a damp rag inside the stovepipe. They are studying the plan and discussing TABARD in BRUEL'S absence.

COLIN: You know, Bruel asked me to allow Tabard into our plan.
CAUSSAT: Tabard's a girl.

THE SCHOOL YARD

The schoolboys are waiting in the courtyard for the signal to go back to their classrooms (drumrolls). They all rush towards the toilets. The HEAD SUPERINTENDENT appears and the boys hastily regroup in rows of two, heading towards the classrooms. The HEAD SUPERINTENDENT disappears (we hear the little tune on the flute).

THE CHEMISTRY CLASS

The boys are up to their usual tricks and the stove is filling the whole classroom with smoke during the chemistry lesson. The teacher is a fat, somewhat pathetic, sweaty, flabby man.
The teacher is trying to give his lesson. He thinks the smoke from the stove is coming from a test-tube and is very worried.

CHEMISTRY TEACHER: Quick! Quick! A container.†

CAUSSAT hands him a funnel.

The following is the version, which was actually filmed and edited, of the chemistry class sequence. CAUSSAT and BRUEL stand near the stove, discussing the plot as they look at their map (seen from above).

* These scenes were not shot.
† According to the essay by P.E. Salès Gomès, Jean Vigo revealed more of the chemistry teacher's personality in the earlier version of the scene. In it, the teacher exclaimed when he saw the smoke and fancied it was a chemical reaction: 'What is the meaning of this reaction? I've been working on it for fifteen years. Somebody's going to be sorry!'

COLIN: Tabard's got a hiding-place.

CAUSSAT: Who? ... Tabard? ... What hiding-place?

COLIN: Don't know.

CAUSSAT: Well, if you don't know you can leave me in peace, you and your Tabard.

COLIN: You wanted him in the plot?

CAUSSAT: Oh! Tabard's a girl, I tell you .... Ever since he went to see the headmaster, I don't know what's got into him. He's a girl, I tell you. What can he do? What does he know?

We hear the sound of the drum out in the courtyard. New shot of the chemistry classroom: CAUSSAT *and* COLIN *quickly fold up their plan and take a seat just as the first pupils come into the room. (The camera is in the last row. We see, from above, the classroom door and, just next to it, a skeleton.)*
The CHEMISTRY TEACHER *comes in last; as he enters the room, the skeleton seems to be following him. The* TEACHER *turns round, puts on his pince-nez to see who is behind him. He then turns to the pupils.*

CHEMISTRY TEACHER: Very very amusing .... I don't like it .... I don't like it one bit!

The teacher puts away his pince-nez and goes over to a coat-stand. As he walks past TABARD, *who sits in the first row, he strokes the boy's long hair.*
Medium close-up of the chemistry teacher taking off his jacket, feeling his armpits and sniffing them, and putting on a working jacket which is even dirtier than the one he has just taken off. He then returns to his desk, picks up his pince-nez and takes a quick look round the class. He embarks on a bizarre sort of toilet: to begin with, he takes out a tube and puts a dab of pomade in each of his nostrils. He then removes his tie with its ready-made knot. He also takes out his handkerchief, which he uses solely to spit in, clearing his throat for this purpose. The camera pans round to TABARD, *as we hear the teacher spitting, off. Quick dissolve to: the* TEACHER, *who has begun his lecture, going up to* TABARD *and stroking his hair again, saying to him in a sugary voice:*

CHEMISTRY TEACHER: Well, little man, aren't we taking notes this morning?

TABARD *nervously pulls out a notebook and starts to write. The* TEACHER *then lays his moist, plump hand on* TABARD'S *left hand (quick close-up).*

CHEMISTRY TEACHER: That's a good boy!

TABARD *snatches his hand away.*

TABARD: Leave me alone!

The CHEMISTRY TEACHER *reacts in a conciliating and at the same time threatening way. He pushes his face right up to* TABARD'S *and says:*

CHEMISTRY TEACHER: Now, my little man, what have you to say?

Exasperated, TABARD *can no longer control himself. He jumps up and stares at the teacher.*

TABARD: What have I to say? I have to say …. Go to hell!

THE OTHER CLASSROOM

Though it is HUGUET *who is watching over the boys, everything is quiet. The atmosphere is tense, solemn. Suddenly, the door opens. The* HEADMASTER, *the* HEAD SUPERINTENDENT, *the* CHEMISTRY TEACHER *and* PARRAIN *walk in, very dignified. The boys and* HUGUET *instantly stand up, and are motioned to sit down again by the* HEADMASTER. *The hostility of the boys towards the masters is shown, and their contempt for* TABARD. CAUSSAT *and* COLIN *are muttering: 'A girl'.* BRUEL *is sad.* HUGUET *appears to be extremely embarrassed.*

The HEADMASTER *puts his bowler hat down on* HUGUET'S *desk.* HUGUET *has remained standing and now walks over to* TABARD *(the camera pans to follow him). Standing behind the* HEADMASTER, *the* CHEMISTRY TEACHER, *the* HEAD SUPERINTENDENT *and* PARRAIN *do their best to look solemn and dignified.*

HEADMASTER: Tabard!

TABARD *gets up.*

HEADMASTER: Tabard, my boy, disciplinary action, you understand ... the board has agreed, under strong pressure by your most kind professor ....

The HEADMASTER *turns towards the* CHEMISTRY TEACHER, *who makes a self-deprecating gesture.*

HEADMASTER: ... You are magnanimous, Mr Viot ... has agreed, as I was saying ... out of consideration for your family, out of kindness towards yourself ....

At that moment, the camera moves about the room from left to right, up to the back of the class, and returns while the HEADMASTER *continues to speak.*

HEADMASTER, *off*: ... and on the occasion of our beloved fête which will be taking place tomorrow ... to forgive you. But, you understand, of course, that you must come, of your own accord ... to beg me to accept your apologies.

The camera pans to HUGUET, *who nervously takes his hat and goes over to the group of masters, standing at a slight distance behind them. The camera returns to the* HEADMASTER, *standing face to face with* TABARD.

HEADMASTER: ... apologies which are worthless if they are not made in public, in front of all your schoolfellows .... We are waiting ....

Disgusted, HUGUET *puts his hat on and is about to leave, not wishing to be a witness to* TABARD's *humiliation.*

HEADMASTER, *growing impatient*: Well! Tell us what you want to say .... *(Silence.)* Tell us what you want to say .... Go on! ....
TABARD *(medium close-up of him)*: I want to say, Sir, I want to say ... go to Hell!

TABARD *sits down again brusquely.*
Fade-out in black.

THE SCHOOL DORMITORY

The dormitory seen from above. The boys are in a state of effervescence. They rush about in their nightshirts. Most of them cluster round TABARD *who is holding his flag with the skull and cross-bones and is reading a proclamation. We can hardly hear him over the din and because he himself is breathless with excitement.*

TABARD: War is declared. Down with the masters! Down with punishment! Long live the rebellion! .... Liberty or death .... Let us plant our flag on the school roof. Tomorrow, we must all be as one man. We swear we will bombard the old jackasses at the fête with old books, old tins, old shoes and ammunition that we've hidden in the loft. Forward! Forward!

TABARD *waves the flag as he moves about the dormitory. All the boys join in and start pulling open the beds.* PARRAIN, *in his nightshirt, stands on a bed trying to make them behave. Numerous shots of children excitedly carrying out their work of destruction.*

THE SCHOOL ROOF

TABARD, *still in his nightshirt, is up on the roof, on all fours. He is fixing the flag to a large chimney.*

THE SCHOOL DORMITORY

Back in the dormitory, the kids are going wild and have started a pillow-fight. The pillows are bursting open under the impact and white feathers scatter in all directions, floating about like snowflakes throughout the room. The beds have been pushed aside and chamber-pots litter the floor. We see PARRAIN *through a thick cloud of feathers, completely exhausted, looking for a chair to sit on. The chair is pulled from under him and he falls over.* *
Quick shot of the door opening: the HEAD SUPERINTENDENT *appears and, when he sees the cloud of feathers, quickly vanishes again.*
Return to a long shot of the dormitory, which is thicker than ever with feathers from the eiderdowns and the pillows.
Just as one boy does a double somersault, landing on the chair

---

* Jean Vigo noted in the script for the composer (Jaubert): 'All this stylised section must be accompanied by an animated cartoon-style music'.

which PARRAIN *had tried to sit on, the film goes into slow motion, emphasising the magic, dreamlike quality of the scene. The music also takes on an eerie quality.*[*]
Behind the acrobat being carried off on his chair, there forms a sort of procession ... still in slow motion. All the children are in a state bordering on ecstasy as the feathers gently rain down on them.
(Each boy in the procession is carrying either a Chinese lantern or a streamer. TABARD *is carrying a T-shaped cross.) At the tail-end of the procession, a tiny ghost: a boy swathed in the curtains that were hung round* PARRAIN'S *bed.*
Fade-out in black and insert on a black background:

'THE NEXT MORNING, EXHAUSTION, / AN ACCOMPLICE OF THE FOUR ...'

Daylight floods the dormitory, which is a mess. The camera tracks sideways along the beds: all the children are fast asleep. The tracking shot ends on a medium close-up of PARRAIN *asleep in his bed, which is no longer hidden now that the curtains have been ripped away. He is sleeping soundly, almost beatifically.*
CAUSSAT, TABARD, BRUEL *and* COLIN *appear, fully dressed. Without waking* PARRAIN, *they tie him up in his bed with a long scarf, raise his bed up so that it is in an upright position, and hang in front of him a twin Chinese lantern which resembles a scale: the scale of Justice, which is blind.*
At that moment, the night watchman walks past the children. He remains impassive and seems to notice nothing amiss.
The four boys immediately prepare their flight to the hiding-place where, for many days, they have been stocking up various provisions. They bundle a few more provisions inside sheets, which they cart off with them. The camera returns to PARRAIN, *still asleep, tied to his bed in a precarious position. A few feathery snowflakes still float about in the air.* PARRAIN *seems to be smiling.*

---

[*] Note by P.E. Salès Gomès: 'To find the perfect musical equivalent of the slow motion images, Jaubert wrote a theme which was recorded backwards and then reversed during montage'.

THE SCHOOL YARD

The school yard is decorated with flags and streamers. A member of the kitchen staff is placing glasses on a trestle table. Near him, the HEAD MASTER *is nervously pacing up and down. The* HEAD SUPERINTENDENT *appears.*

HEAD SUPERINTENDENT: Sir, the children have locked themselves up in the attic.[*]

HEADMASTER, *raising his arms to Heaven*: It's astonishing … I've never heard of anything like it before!

Quick shot in which the camera follows the PRIEST *as he runs over to greet the important people (including the* PREFECT) *who are making their way to the dais which has been erected for them.*

PRIEST, *to the* PREFECT: Oh Sir, Sir! …. What a fête! Good Lord, what a fête!

We follow the PRIEST *as he runs over to the* HEADMASTER.

PRIEST, *to the* HEADMASTER: The honourable Prefect has just taken a seat …. The honourable Prefect is sitting down.

He goes off again; the HEADMASTER *too goes over to the dais. Sideways tracking shot of the flag-bedecked school yard: in the foreground, a fireman (seen from the back) standing to attention. Another fireman is performing exercises on a wooden horse. Between the two firemen, in the background, we can see the officials sitting on the dais in the first row. In the second row are horrible puppets from a fairground shooting gallery. Everyone looks very dignified. The tracking shot ends on the seated pupils. Near them,* HUGUET, *who looks up at the roof and sees the flag with the skull painted on it. Long shot of the school yard, seen from above, then a shot of the four boys* CAUSSAT, COLIN, BRUEL, TABARD *on the roof, near the flag.*

---

[*] Though Vigo specifically mentioned that this was to be a silent part, it is the Head Superintendent who breaks the news to the Headmaster. According to P.E. Salès Gomès, in the original version the officials looked worried because they knew already that the four young rebels had locked themselves up in the attic.

Quick shot of the HEAD SUPERINTENDENT, *sitting in the first row next to the* HEADMASTER. *He gets up and, with his very characteristic walk, he heads towards the latrines.*
We return to the four children up on the roof. They suddenly begin to hurl missiles at the officials on the dais. Different shots of the kids throwing their missiles and of their pals below, encouraging them (including HUGUET). *Shots of the officials trying to shield themselves from the missiles. Egged on by* HUGUET, *all the boys now start joining in the game of hurling missiles, while the officials and the firemen rush towards the school buildings, heading for the attic. The* HEAD SUPERINTENDENT *follows them and turns for a second, giving a wry grin, almost a smile of satisfaction.*
Again we have a long shot of the courtyard, seen from the roof. The four kids stop hurling their missiles. HUGUET, *surrounded by all the boys, raises his arms up in the air as though to hail the rebels' victory.*
Quick shot of the four children waving the flag and throwing it down to their pals.

THE ATTIC

The PREFECT *and the* HEADMASTER *follow the two firemen, who have broken down the door into the attic. Behind them come* PARRAIN *and the* HEAD SUPERINTENDENT.
Quick shot of the four rebel boys (seen from the back) as they climb up the roof, singing.
The HEADMASTER *rushes over to the skylight, followed by the* PREFECT.
They look out and see:
Slow shot of the children on the roof, climbing, climbing, climbing ever higher … as the words THE END *appear on the screen.*

THE END

L'ATALANTE

(1934)

L'ATALANTE

Music and screen credits over medium close-up of a barge in the mist with the name L'Atalante painted very legibly on its hull.

After the credits, the film opens on a long shot of the motorbarge L'Atalante which lies seemingly deserted along a river bank in the middle of the countryside; there is no one and nothing else in sight.

Cut to long shot of a village square with a little church. The music stops.

Medium close-up of the church door. PÈRE JULES *and* THE KID *come running out, dressed up in their Sunday best.*

PÈRE JULES: Come on, hurry! Hurry!

PÈRE JULES and THE KID start to run across the village square. PÈRE JULES stops abruptly, as though he has forgotten something, and turns back. THE KID starts to follow him, then stops, a look of surprise on his face.

PÈRE JULES reaches the church door, dips a finger in the holy water, makes the sign of the cross and runs off again.

PÈRE JULES returns to the spot where THE KID is still standing and they both set off again, running as fast as they can.

Medium shot of the church door. We hear music and the muffled sound of voices. First the bride and the groom emerge from the church, with solemn expressions on their faces. They are followed by all the wedding guests, first two children, then the bride's mother. A crowd of onlookers has stopped outside the church to stare at the proceedings.

A WEDDING GUEST: Now, now, mother! You can't complain. She's found a fine fellow. She'll come back some day, she will!

THE MOTHER: When I think that she's never so much as set foot outside the village!

Long shot of the wedding group walking alongside the church. Two men play the accordion. The last guest in the procession jokingly slaps the behind of the man just in front of him.

ANOTHER WEDDING GUEST: Pity they couldn't give a wedding party. I always enjoy that.

Medium tracking shot of the wedding group. One of the guests is trying to arrange the procession in a more orderly fashion.

ANOTHER GUEST: I hear they've got to get a move on. They're late already.

ANOTHER GUEST: He said he'd get into trouble with the Waterways people.

ANOTHER GUEST: What's his name?

Music.

ANOTHER GUEST: The groom's name? I've forgotten, but I know the boat's called l'Atalante.

ANOTHER GUEST: Well, are we going back with them to the barge by the shortcut?

ANOTHER GUEST: What a long way for a fellow we don't even know.

ANOTHER GUEST: Why couldn't she marry a village boy?

ANOTHER GUEST: She never did do like the others. She don't like our village any more.

ANOTHER GUEST: *trying to organise the procession*: Hurry up! Hey, Toinette, are you coming or not? Stand right there, you! Get a move on, will you! The bride and groom are at the far end of the village already.

The wedding guests fall silent and look at the bride and groom who are disappearing down a side street. The guests start running after them, past the camera.
Cut to PÈRE JULES *and* THE KID *running across a field. They reach a steep slope; the boy scrambles up, effortlessly, but* PÈRE JULES *stumbles and slips and has to use his hands to get to the top. Cut to rapid shot of the wedding group, then cut back to* PÈRE JULES *and* THE KID, *seen from above, as they reach the barge.*

PÈRE JULES: What about your speech, eh?

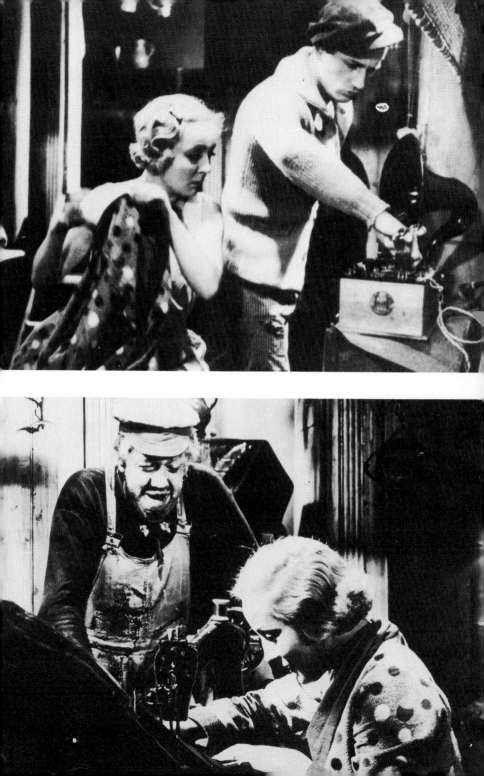

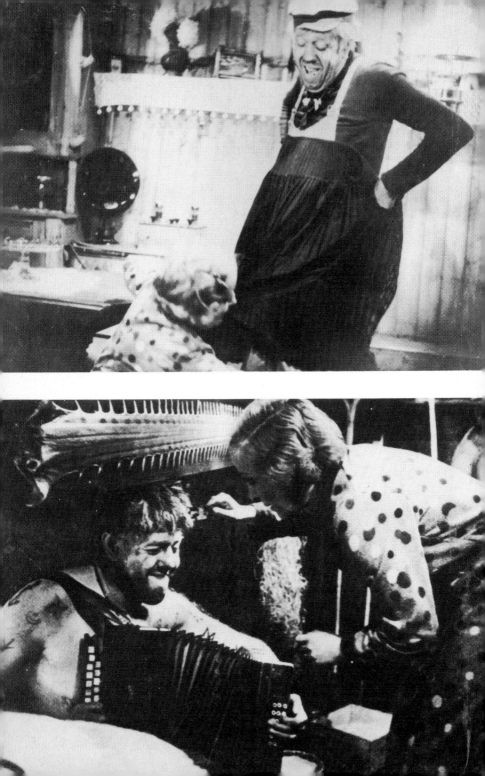

THE KID: Sure ... Sure ....

PÈRE JULES: *sceptical*: You know it? You know it? What about the bride? What are you going to say to the bride?

THE KID: What you told me to say to her.

PÈRE JULES: What I told you ... Well, what did I tell you?

> *Cut to the bride and groom walking arm in arm down a street. They are alone and seem very calm and happy. The bride is wearing a white wedding-dress and a veil. The groom looks a trifle awkward in his Sunday suit, as though he were far more accustomed to wearing a polo-necked jersey than a shirt and a tie. We can hear the music of the accordions, muffled at first, then growing louder as the wedding party catches up with the newly married pair. The guests now walk a little way behind the couple; they are a noisy, cheerful lot and their mood is in striking contrast to the quiet serenity of the young man and woman.*
>
> *The camera tracks slowly back as the wedding group advances. Then the camera stops and the procession walks across the screen, towards the left. Finally, the camera pans at a 180° angle to catch the group once again, now seen from behind. The wedding party recedes, disappearing from view as it climbs up a slope.*
>
> *New shot of a gently sloping field; we catch sight of the bride and the groom again, a long way away, as they walk towards the camera, then past the camera which remains still, then off again.*
>
> *Cut back to* PÈRE JULES *and* THE KID, *still panting from their exertions, standing on the deck of the barge.* PÈRE JULES *picks up a kitten and puts it on his shoulder; he then goes to another part of the deck to fetch a second cat which he cradles in his arms. He starts to feed both cats titbits which he takes out of his pockets and, while he strokes the cats, he speaks to* THE KID .

PÈRE JULES: Well, d'you understand?

THE KID: Oh sure, sure!

PÈRE JULES: Sure, sure! That's not an answer. What do you do when they get here? I've been coaching you for ten whole days.

THE KID: I go up to the boss's wife, I give her the flowers and I say ...

PÈRE JULES: What do you say?

THE KID: I say: 'Here's to a happy life aboard l'Atalante'.

PÈRE JULES: All right. That'll do. Have you got the flowers?

THE KID: They're still in the bucket.

The boy goes off as PÈRE JULES *watches him. Shot of* THE KID *pulling on a string which is tied to a bucket, floating in the river, containing a bunch of flowers.* PÈRE JULES *comes into shot, the kitten still perched on his shoulder. We can hear the music in the distance.*

PÈRE JULES: Put some paper round them or else she'll get her dress wet.

We hear the music of the accordion-players in the wedding group more clearly now. PÈRE JULES *and the boy listen and then look towards the bank.*

PÈRE JULES *and* THE KID *together*: Here they come! Here they come!

PÈRE JULES *takes his accordion, which is lying on the deck, and starts to play. The music of his accordion seems to answer the distant music of the wedding party as it comes nearer.* PÈRE JULES *dances as he plays and* THE KID *starts to dance, too.*
Quick insert of the wedding group, led by the bride and groom, as they walk swiftly through a thicket.
Cut back to the barge: the kid, as he dances, knocks over the bucket which falls back into the water with the flowers still in it. PÈRE JULES'S *accordion stops abruptly, but we can still hear the music of the other accordions.* THE KID *falls flat on his stomach in an attempt to catch the flowers.* PÈRE JULES *swoops down on him. The camera tracks rapidly down onto* THE KID *lying on the deck and trying to hold onto the bucket by the string.* PÈRE JULES *comes into shot and also falls onto his stomach to help retrieve the string. We can hear the music getting closer.*

PÈRE JULES: I knew it! It had to happen!

THE KID: I've got the string. I've got it.

PÈRE JULES: The string …. To hell with the string! Give it here.

PÈRE JULES *and* THE KID *grab at the string and manage to*

draw the bucket out of the water, but the flowers have already floated out of the bucket. Furious, PÈRE JULES *throws the water in the bucket at* THE KID. *The flowers start to float away in the current.* PÈRE JULES'S *cap suddenly appears next to the flowers: it has obviously fallen into the water as* PÈRE JULES *was bending over to look at the bouquet. Shot of* PÈRE JULES, *looking depressed but fatalistic at this final stroke of ill-luck.* THE KID *looks extremely despondent.*

PÈRE JULES: There it goes.

The camera tilts slightly upwards on the two as they lean over the edge of the barge to look down at the water. PÈRE JULES *is bare-headed now, but the kitten is still perched on his shoulder.* THE KID *then stares at* PÈRE JULES *in dismay.*

THE KID: I've got some money. I'll go get another bunch.
PÈRE JULES: You must be joking! We're in the middle of nowhere and they're coming now. Forget it.

THE KID *jumps off the boat and leaves shot.* PÈRE JULES, *worried, looks at him go and gets up, still holding the empty pail which he tosses across the deck.*

PÈRE JULES, *calling out to the Kid*: Hey! Where are you going? It doesn't matter!

THE KID *scrambles up the river bank, then turns and waves to* PÈRE JULES *before disappearing from sight.*

THE KID, *shouting*: I'll go and pick some!

PÈRE JULES *is reassured, but his expression remains morose as he looks at the wedding party appearing in the distance. Music. Insert of* THE KID *looking for flowers to pick, then cut back to the deck of the barge.* PÈRE JULES *sits down and starts giving titbits to his cats. Cut to the wedding party walking through the thicket.*
Shot of THE KID *looking for non-existent flowers along the stony river bank.*
Shot of PÈRE JULES *sitting on the edge of the deck. Insert: medium close-up of the bouquet floating downstream.* PÈRE JULES *catches sight of it, tries to snatch it back but fails. He then*

puts two fingers to his mouth and whistles.
THE KID *reappears at the top of the river bank, peeping like a faun through an armful of foliage he has picked. The camera pans after him as he runs down to the river's edge.*

PÈRE JULES'S *voice*: Over there! Quick! The flowers! Don't fall in!

THE KID *jumps into the small rowboat which is tied to the back of the barge, catches the bouquet and leaps back onto the river bank, triumphantly waving the flowers.*
Shot of the wedding group, now very close to the barge.

PÈRE JULES'S *voice*: Put some paper round them!

THE KID *comes into shot and shoves the wet bouquet into the bride's arms. The bride holds the soaking flowers.*

THE KID: Here's to a happy life aboard l'Atalante!

Cut to PÈRE JULES standing on the river bank, waiting. JEAN, the groom, walks up to the spot where he stands.

PÈRE JULES: Are we leaving right away, boss?
JEAN: Of course we are. I told you so already.
PÈRE JULES: Right. I'll go and warm up the engine.

They move off together.
Medium close-up of JULIETTE, the bride, holding the flowers and standing on the river bank, a sad look on her face.
Cut to JEAN on deck, changing into his working clothes.
Cut back to JULIETTE on the river bank. She is standing in the foreground, clutching her bouquet. The wedding guests, in the background, also stand quite still and look on, disapprovingly. The music has stopped and we now hear the sound of the barge's engine instead.
JEAN is already standing at the helm. The barge is ready to leave. The wedding guests, now minus the bride, stand and watch.

JEAN, *at the helm, shouting*: Hey! Patronne!

The motor rumbles. Long shot of PÈRE JULES and the bride standing next to the barge; beyond them, the bride's relatives

96

and friends. PÈRE JULES *helps the bride to climb aboard and takes her flowers. We now see the bride standing near the mast as her mother rushes forward.*

THE MOTHER: Juliette! Juliette!

We hear the sound of the barge engine. PÈRE JULES, *still standing on the river bank, catches the mother in his arms, gives her a kiss and thrusts the bouquet in her arms; he then goes up to the boat but, changing his mind, he takes the flowers back.*

PÈRE JULES, *to the mother*: There she is. There's your daughter.

PÈRE JULES *clambers onto the boat. Sound of the boat engine. Insert of* THE KID *drawing in the rowboat at the back.*
The bride is now standing alone in the stern of l'Atalante. We see her from behind. Music throughout the following sequence.
Close-up of PÈRE JULES, *now wearing a striped sweater, using a boat hook.*
Shot of JEAN *at the helm, very happy and waving goodbye cheerfully to the wedding party on the bank.*
Shot of the group of people standing on the river bank, as if seen from the barge which is gliding away.
Shot of the barge as it moves away from the bank.
Insert of a country cottage, its windows lighting up.
Shot of the barge as seen from the river bank. JEAN, PÈRE JULES *and* THE KID *are all hard at work, though they find time to wave to the guests.*
JEAN *waves to them, standing alone at the helm.*
Insert of clouds in the sky.
The wind blows, the guests look up at the sky and start walking home.
Cut back to JULIETTE *standing motionless at the back of the barge, seen slightly from below. The sky is grey. It is dusk. The wind is blowing.*
JEAN *creeps up to where* JULIETTE *is standing and catches her in his arms. They fall down onto the deck,* JULIETTE *struggling. It is almost night now. The music has stopped.*

JULIETTE, *in a whisper*: Where have you come from?

Just then, a cat brushes against JULIETTE, *scaring her. She cries out and jumps up. The cat leaps at* JEAN *and scratches his face.*

JEAN, *crest-fallen*: Don't be scared! Those are Père Jules's work cats.

Night has completely fallen by now. The wind still blows and the music starts again. The barge moves through the night. We can see the bride, in her white dress, walking along the deck. The camera tracks alongside the boat, following her.
Insert of JEAN *calling out to* JULLIETTE, *then cut back to* JULIETTE *walking even faster. Music.*
The camera tilts up to reveal an old woman standing on the river bank with a child, outlined by the cloudy sky. The old woman crosses herself.
The bride stands at the front of the boat now, her white dress blowing in the breeze. JEAN *runs after her, but he stumbles on some ropes and falls down. One of* PÈRE JULES'S *cats jumps at him out of the darkness.*
JULIETTE *turns to look at her husband who is shooing away the cats.*
Insert of JEAN, *a look of dismay on his face, then long shot of the barge with* PÈRE JULES *and* JULIETTE *standing a little way away from* JEAN. *Wind.*
JEAN *finally reaches* JULIETTE *and firmly catches her; she does not struggle but allows him to pick her up and to carry her off, past* PÈRE JULES *and* THE KID. *As they go past, she covers him with kisses. The music stops.*
Fade out.
Fade in on the deck of l'Atalante. It is morning and the sun shines brightly. JEAN *is at the helm;* PÈRE JULES *and* THE KID *seem to be waiting for someone. They exchange glances and grin at each other like two accomplices. Suddenly,* JULIETTE *emerges from the cabin.*

THE KID: Here she comes!

PÈRE JULES *grabs his accordion as the camera tracks back to show* JEAN, THE KID *and* PÈRE JULES *who all start singing the Boatmen's Song.*
Insert of JULIETTE *blinking in the bright sunshine and looking at them with delight.*

Shot of PÈRE JULES *and* THE KID *singing the song; then* PÈRE JULES *goes over to the helm while* THE KID *picks up the accordion and continues to play the song.* JEAN *walks over to* JULIETTE *and helps her up onto the deck.*

JEAN *holds* JULIETTE *in his arms and whispers something in her ear. She snuggles up to him happily and they start exchanging endearments and caresses. Their manner is completely different today from what it was the previous day when they were relatively undemonstrative with each other.*

 *

JULIETTE, *who would have liked to find herself alone with* JEAN, *goes off again.* JEAN, PÈRE JULES *and* THE KID *watch her go, startled by her departure. They have stopped singing.*

PÈRE JULES: Well, well. Botched it, I guess.

JULIETTE *is sitting by herself a little way away, her back turned to the three men. She is trying to sing the song of the Boatmen to herself, though she can only remember a few words of it.* JEAN *goes over to where she sits and notices that she is trying to sing the song. He puts his lips close to* JULIETTE'S *ear and we hear them both as they sing the song together.*

PÈRE JULES'S *voice, off*: They're here! They're here!

At the sound of PÈRE JULES'S *voice,* JEAN *and* JULIETTE *stop singing and* JULIETTE *goes back into the cabin.*
Shot of PÈRE JULES *at the helm, gesticulating and looking through binoculars.* JEAN *takes his place at the helm.*

PÈRE JULES: They've come! They're waiting for me!

The barge moves closer to the river bank. PÈRE JULES *walks towards camera until he stands in close-up.*
The camera tracks sideways to show three cats waiting on the bank.
PÈRE JULES, *standing on the deck, starts to throw bits of meat to the cats; he then jumps off the boat to be with the animals.*

---

* The following scene is not included in the final version of the film.

PÈRE JULES: Here, pussy, pussy! They've come, the little dears. Well, I never! Just look at that!

L_____J

JULIETTE *emerges from the cabin once again.*

JULIETTE: Jean!

JEAN *immediately comes into shot and calls out to* PÈRE JULES *angrily.*
JULIETTE *catches sight of* PÈRE JULES *who also comes into shot carrying one cat on his shoulder and the other in his arms.*

JULIETTE, *to* PÈRE JULES: So there you are. You and your cats. Come and have a look.

All three go down into the cabin.
Inside the cabin, JEAN, JULIETTE *and* PÈRE JULES, *who still carries his cats, walk over to the bed which remains out of sight.*

JULIETTE: Just look!

The three people stop.

PÈRE JULES: Oh! Minoune's had her babies!

Shot of the cat with its kittens, lying on the bed.

JEAN: On our bed? You're going too far!

PÈRE JULES *walks up to the bed, kisses the mother cat and picks up a kitten.*

PÈRE JULES: Well, I'm not their father. *(to* JULIETTE*)* Look!

He thrusts the kitten in her face. She jumps back and JEAN *pushes* PÈRE JULES *out of the way.*

JEAN: Go on! Get them out of here or I'll throw the lot in the water!

PÈRE JULES *hurls himself on the kittens and hastily starts to shove them into his pockets. He even picks one up with his teeth.*

100

PÈRE JULES: Into the water? You'd drown your own kid, you would! Here, Minoune, come along.

PÈRE JULES leaves the cabin. JULIETTE tidies up the bed.

JEAN, *smiling*: You know, Juliette, he's got three more cats.
JULIETTE, *holding the bedspread*: Where do you keep the dirty laundry?
JEAN: Over there, in the wardrobe.

Medium close-up of the tiny wardrobe. JULIETTE comes into shot and opens the wardrobe doors. Dirty laundry spills out of the wardrobe, which is filled to overflowing. A cat leaps out.

JULIETTE: How often do you wash the laundry? Once a year?
JEAN, *coming into shot*: Not that often.

They both smile. JEAN picks up one of the cats and strokes it.

JULIETTE: Well, it's going to be different from now on.

She opens a bag full of laundry and starts to empty its contents.

JEAN: Wait until tomorrow.
JULIETTE: Why should I?
JEAN: Just because. Not today. You know, there's plenty of time here.
JULIETTE: No. No.
JEAN: All right, I'll help you then.

JEAN picks up the dirty laundry and starts walking towards the cabin stairs.
PÈRE JULES'S cabin. The room is full of fishing tackle, exotic souvenirs from the four corners of the world and old knick-knacks of bygone days. There are two bunks, one for PÈRE JULES and the other for THE KID. The cabin is full of cats. PÈRE JULES is looking after the mother and her newborn kittens. THE KID comes in and sees the cat, lying comfortably on the bed which PÈRE JULES has prepared for her.

THE KID: I've come to collect the dirty laundry. Oh! Look at Minoune and her babies!
PÈRE JULES: The dirty laundry? What for?
THE KID: The boss's wife is going to wash it.

PÈRE JULES *laughing*: The boss's wife wants to wash my dirty laundry?

> JULIETTE *and* JEAN *up on the deck, standing near the washtub.* THE KID *comes into shot and gives* JULIETTE *his small bundle of dirty laundry.*

THE KID: Père Jules refuses to give his laundry.
JEAN: He does?
PÈRE JULES *off*: Yes he does!

> JEAN, JULIETTE *and* THE KID *turn to stare at* PÈRE JULES *who is carrying a bundle of laundry.*

PÈRE JULES: I don't need anyone. I learned how to wash my own feet long before I ever met you!
JEAN, *going up to* PÈRE JULES: Don't be an ass. Give it to me.

> PÈRE JULES *hesitates, then gives the bundle of laundry to* JEAN.

PÈRE JULES: Well all right, if you insist. I'm only doing it to please the boss's wife.

> *A whistle blows.* PÈRE JULES *turns and goes to the upper deck.*

⎡‾‾‾‾‾‾‾‾‾‾‾‾‾‾⎤ *

> A TRAMP, *is waving to* PÈRE JULES.
> PÈRE JULES *goes ashore to talk to* THE TRAMP.

PÈRE JULES: Hullo there, Rasputin!
THE TRAMP: I've got a record.
PÈRE JULES: Is it a long one?
THE TRAMP: Have a look for yourself!

> THE TRAMP *hands the record to* PÈRE JULES.

PÈRE JULES: Well, if you must know, I haven't finished fixing my gramophone yet. There's a spring missing, a spring and also … how much do you want for this flapjack, anyway?
THE TRAMP: Twenty *sous*.

* The following sequence was not included in the final version.

PÈRE JULES: Are you crazy? Ten.
THE TRAMP: I'd rather eat it.

PÈRE JULES hesitates. THE KID *comes into shot.*

PÈRE JULES, *to the Kid*: Have you got twenty *sous*?

THE KID *gives him the money and* PÈRE JULES *buys the record.*

PÈRE JULES: And what about the junk?
THE TRAMP: Oh yes, I'd forgotten you liked that stuff. I've got some. Let's go and look at it.

PÈRE JULES *and* THE KID *go off with* THE TRAMP.
JULIETTE *and* JEAN *at the washtub.*

THE TRAMP: Now that Père Jean has met a pal of his, he'll be bamboozled again. He's always buying or picking up bits of junk, old springs, spare parts, that sort of muck.

PÈRE JULES, THE KID *and* THE TRAMP *are looking at some junk which is set out on the pavement next to a grocery belonging to a short-sighted grocer.* PÈRE JULES *is putting all kinds of odds and ends into his bag: an empty gramophone case, some horseshoes, etc.*

THE JUNK DEALER: Ten *sous*.
PÈRE JULES: Five.
THE JUNK DEALER: Right. It's a deal.
PÈRE JULES: How about this one, Rasputin?
THE JUNK DEALER: Done. You can have it.
PÈRE JULES: How about this one, Rasputin?
THE TRAMP: Depends.

PÈRE JULES *has noticed that* THE KID *is stealing an orange from the short-sighted greengrocer's display outside the shop. The grocer is cleaning his spectacles.*
THE KID *steals a second orange.*
The grocer, still wiping his spectacles.
PÈRE JULES, *as he goes on buying junk from the dealer, watches* THE KID *out of the corner of his eye and sees him taking a third orange while the grocer stands outside his shop, wiping his glasses.*

PÈRE JULES, *aside, to* THE KID: Hey you, come over here.

THE KID *looks sheepish under the stern gaze of* PÈRE JULES.

PÈRE JULES: You know what you are? A thief, that's what. It's wrong to steal. What if everyone did it?

> *Meanwhile, the* JUNK DEALER *is surreptitiously removing something from* PÈRE JULES'S *bag.* THE TRAMP *looks at the* JUNK DEALER *reproachfully so that he quickly takes a second item out of* PÈRE JULES'S *bag and gives it to* THE TRAMP. THE KID *and* PÈRE JULES.

PÈRE JULES: Open your bag. Three oranges? But there's four of us! Come, you know you might as well be hanged for a sheep as for a lamb and for four oranges instead of three.

> PÈRE JULES *picks up his bag as he walks past the* JUNK DEALER *and filches a fourth orange from the greengrocer's shop.*
> JULIETTE *and* JEAN *are hanging up the clean laundry on lines strung across the deck of the barge.* JEAN *empties the washtub and starts to fill it again with clean water which he draws from the bucket.*
> PÈRE JULES *and* THE KID, *carrying a shopping bag full of food, stop outside a butcher's shop.*

PÈRE JULES, *calling out*: Hullo there! Mrs Jules?
THE WOMAN INSIDE THE SHOP: Hello there, Monsieur Jules.
PÈRE JULES: Can I have some scraps for my cats?
THE WOMAN: The usual sort?
PÈRE JULES: Naturally.

> THE WOMAN *comes out of the shop, holding a big chunk of meat which she is wrapping up.* PÈRE JULES *and* THE KID *go off again.*

⌐￢

> *On the deck of* l'Atalante, JEAN *is bending over a bucket full of water, washing himself. He is stripped to the waist.* JULIETTE *playfully pushes his head down into the bucket. She laughs as* JEAN *raises his head with tightly-shut eyes.*

104

JULIETTE: Oh! You shut your eyes.

JEAN: Of course I did. I wasn't expecting you to do that. Besides, it doesn't matter.

JULIETTE: Don't you know that you can see your beloved's face under the water?

JEAN: What do you mean?

JULIETTE: It's really true! I saw lots of things under the water when I was little, and last year I saw you. That's why I recognised you straight away that day you came to my house for the first time.

JEAN: Is that true?

He plunges his head into the bucket again, then takes it out.

JEAN: I didn't see a thing. Wait a moment.

He runs across the deck and plunges his head over the side into the river. JULIETTE *dashes after him.*

JULIETTE: Jean!

JEAN'S *head is completely immersed in water.* JULIETTE *is amused but a trifle anxious because he remains with his head in the river for so long. He finally pulls it out, only to plunge it in again immediately.*

JULIETTE: No, stop it! Take your head out. Are you crazy? I don't want you to do it. It's only a game.

JEAN, *each time he draws his head out*: I can't see you.

JEAN: Ah! Now I see you.

*JULIETTE crossly moves away from him. JEAN follows her.
JEAN runs after JULIETTE all over the deck, and in and out of the washing which is hung out to dry. They seem to be playing hide and seek.
PÈRE JULES and THE KID are coming back from the town, their arms laden with purchases, food, junk, horseshoes, etc.
JEAN catches JULIETTE and tries to hold her; they struggle as he grabs one of her arms and tries to put it through his. JULIETTE starts to escape and they end up standing back to back. JEAN catches JULIETTE'S other arm and lifts her off the ground in this fashion. JULIETTE, still trying to get away, lifts JEAN off the ground as they both laugh.*

PÈRE JULES, *who has returned, looks at* JEAN *and* JULIETTE *playing. He puts down his bag and his record.* THE KID *takes all the junk down into the cabin.*
JEAN *and* JULIETTE *stop playing when they see* PÈRE JULES *walking towards them.*

PÈRE JULES, *scornfully*: Well, if that's the best you can do! Personally, I prefer the technique of Paul Pons and Raoul the Butcher. Those fellows really knew a thing or two about boxing.

PÈRE JULES *takes up a boxing stance and starts to fight with an imaginary adversary.* JEAN *and* JULIETTE *slip off while* PÈRE JULES, *who still thinks he is giving a demonstration in boxing technique, mimes two boxers locked in a ferocious struggle.*

PÈRE JULES: And a hook to the right ... And another to the left ....

Inside their cabin, JEAN *finishes drying himself, helped by* JULIETTE.
Fade-out.

        ⌐￣￣￣￣￣￣￣￣¬   *

The empty deck of l'Atalante as the barge moves swiftly through the countryside. We hear its motor chugging steadily.
The empty deck of l'Atalante as it moves in the rain.
The empty deck of l'Atalante at dusk, fading to:
The empty deck of l'Atalante at night.

JULIETTE *lies alone in her cabin bed.*

JULIETTE, *calling to* JEAN: Jean! Are you coming down?

There is no reply. JULIETTE *gets up and leaves the cabin.*
The open deck of l'Atalante. It is night. JULIETTE *emerges from the cabin and sees* JEAN *at the helm.*

JULIETTE: Jean, it's eleven o'clock. When are you going to stop?
JEAN: It's not my fault, is it?

* These shots were cut out of the final version.

PÈRE JULES *comes to take* JEAN'S *place at the helm.*

PÈRE JULES: Your wife is right. Go to bed. She needs more than a blanket to keep warm.

> JULIETTE, *inside the cabin, is getting back into bed.*

JULIETTE: And to think it's like this every evening.

> *The deck of l'Atalante. Night.* PÈRE JULES *is standing at the helm as the motor chugs away. Fade to:*
> *The deck of l'Atalante at dawn.*
> *Inside the cabin,* JEAN *is getting dressed.* JULIETTE, *who is already dressed, stands next to him, handing him his clothes. She then picks up her knitting and starts to measure* JEAN'S *arms and chest.*

JEAN: Are you knitting another sweater?
JULIETTE: What else is there to do?

> *She gets up, goes over to the wardrobe and takes out a clean jumper for* JEAN.

JEAN: Are you bored?
JULIETTE, *without much conviction*: Oh no!
JEAN, *getting up*: We'll move on and you'll see a bit more country that way.
JULIETTE: More river banks? Listen, when do we arrive?
JEAN, *turning round*: Arrive where?
JULIETTE: Oh, I don't know. Wherever you fancy. (JEAN *goes off*) Somewhere. A city. A big city. How long does it take to unload in a big city?

> *As* JEAN *walks past the radio set in the cabin, he turns the dial and we hear various radio sounds while the camera tracks towards the set.*

RADIO: Radio Paris ....

> JULIETTE *listens to the radio; she puts the jumper back in the wardrobe and eagerly walks up to the set. As she moves, she goes past* JEAN *who is still dressing and not interested in the broadcast.*

RADIO: Radio Paris ....

JULIETTE, *sitting down to listen*: Jean! It's Paris!

JEAN: What?

JULIETTE: Paris.

JEAN: So what? Are you surprised?

JULIETTE: Are we far away?

JEAN: Near or far, we'd still hear it clearly.

JULIETTE: I'm asking you if Paris is far because I want to know how long it'll take us to get there.

JEAN: Oh, one is never far enough from those Paris docks. They ain't much fun.

RADIO: Hello. Radio Paris speaking. The latest fashion bulletin .... For another two weeks, on the Boulevard Haussman, there will be displays in all the windows of ....

JEAN comes into shot and turns the dial to find another station.

JEAN: Talk, talk, talk.

The radio now plays some jazz music.

JULIETTE: Don't! Leave it on Paris!

She starts to turn the radio dial back to the Paris station. JEAN, annoyed, is also afraid that she will break his set, and he pushes her away quite roughly. JULIETTE crossly pushes him out of the way.
JEAN is furious by now, but he manages to control his anger.

JULIETTE: Do be careful. You know there's hardly enough room to move here.

JEAN turns the set off and sits down. The various radio noises stop abruptly. JULIETTE turns the dial on again and finds the Paris station.

RADIO: The fashionable colour this year is burgundy red. Lamé, velvet and satin, as usual, predominate for evening wear. Radio Paris speaking.

The deck of l'Atalante at dawn. JEAN, as usual, is standing at the helm. PÈRE JULES takes over from him. We hear the Paris radio signal. Fade out.
Fog. L'Atalante moves closer to the river bank. Insert of a tramp waving to PÈRE JULES.

THE KID *takes over from* JEAN *at the helm.*

JEAN, *to* PÈRE JULES: Turn the lights on and don't fall into the river. I'm just going to find my wife, then I'll be back.

> JEAN *in the cabin. He sees that* JULIETTE *is not there and rushes out again.*
> THE KID *alone, up on the deck. We hear foghorns blowing through the rising fog.*
> JEAN *emerges from the cabin.*

JEAN: My wife! Where is she? *(calling out)* Juliette!

> *We hear the echo of her name as he calls it out.*
> JEAN, *looking for* JULIETTE *on the deck, in the fog.*
> PÈRE JULES *meets* JEAN *on the deck.*

JEAN, *calling*: Juliette!

> JEAN *gropes his way through the thick fog like a blind man.*
> JULIETTE *is up on the deck, but she neither moves nor speaks.*
> JEAN *finds her and they embrace. They walk off, clasping each other.* JEAN *gives her a gentle shake and kisses her.*

JEAN: Why didn't you answer? I was worried.

> *The camera tracks after* JEAN *and* JULIETTE *as they walk past* PÈRE JULES. PÈRE JULES, *who is still anxious, rushes up to them.*

PÈRE JULES: What was the matter?
JEAN: Nothing.
PÈRE JULES: What do you mean, nothing?

> JEAN *sweeps past* PÈRE JULES, *leading* JULIETTE *down into the cabin.*

JEAN: Leave us alone.
PÈRE JULES: What?

> JEAN *turns to look at* PÈRE JULES *just before disappearing into the cabin.*

JEAN: Go and work.

> *The cabin hatch closes in* PÈRE JULES'S *face.* PÈRE JULES

heads for his cabin, a cat on one shoulder.

PÈRE JULES, *grumbling*: Work! What next? They're starting to get on my nerves, those two. Maybe it's that Juliette of his who greases the engine .... They spend their whole time either kissing or squabbling .... Well, if that's how it is I can always leave. I don't feel at home here.

He jumps down onto the river bank.
PÈRE JULES, *walking away in the fog.*

 *

PÈRE JULES *hears a cat miaowling; he stops and looks around. Two cats near a fence. One of them is behind the fence, the other is on the outside.*

PÈRE JULES: What? Why, it's Zigomar! Are you going courting? And what about you, you vixen? You must get some pretty decent chow in a dump like this one.

PÈRE JULES *looks at the nameplate on the gate of the villa.*

PÈRE JULES: What's your master's name? What? He's a judge, is he? In that case, you'd better come with me!

He goes off with both cats.

JULIETTE *and* JEAN *are sitting at table in their cabin with* THE KID. *They have just finished eating their dinner.* PÈRE JULES *has not turned up for the meal.*

JEAN: Do you think he's angry?
JULIETTE: Of course not.
JEAN: Then where's he gone?
JULIETTE: He won't go far. Stop worrying. You'll see your Père Jules again.

* This brief scene was cut out of the final version.

110

At that moment, PÈRE JULES *comes in and sits down. He starts to eat, one cat on each knee. There is an awkward silence.*

JEAN: Why didn't you show up at the usual time?

PÈRE JULES *does not reply. He eats hastily, giving scraps to both cats. Finally he looks up at* JEAN *and* JULIETTE.
JULIETTE'S *head is resting on* JEAN'S *shoulder. The two young people are both looking at* PÈRE JULES, *off, smiling fondly at him. The camera tracks to:*
PÈRE JULES *eating sulkily.* JEAN *would like to break the ice somehow. He slaps* PÈRE JULES *on the shoulder; finally,* PÈRE JULES *grins.*

JEAN: Come on! Don't sulk. Shall we have a drink?

We hear the foghorn of a boat in the distance. The camera follows JEAN *as he gets up.*

JEAN: Well, I guess the fog must be lifting. We'd better get a move on and make up for lost time.

PÈRE JULES *gets up and the three men leave the cabin.*

┌─────────────────────┐ *

JULIETTE *remains alone in the cabin, sitting on the bed. We hear the engine of l'Atalante starting up.*
JEAN *stands at the helm. The barge is on its way once more.*
JEAN *bends over to talk to* PÈRE JULES *down below in the engine room through a special microphone installed there for that purpose. We hear the roar of the engine.*

JEAN: Well, Père Jules?

PÈRE JULES, *down in the engine room, holding an oiling can in one hand, a rather disenchanted expression on his face.*

JEAN'S *voice:* Everything all right?

└─────────────────────┘

---

* This scene was cut out of the final version.

JULIETTE *gets up and goes over to her sewing machine.* PÈRE
JULES *comes in and goes over to where she sits, working.*
PÈRE JULES *standing near* JULIETTE *who is stitching a skirt on
the machine.*

PÈRE JULES: What are you making?
JULIETTE: I'm sewing. Haven't you ever seen a sewing machine
before?

PÈRE JULES *sits down next to* JULIETTE, *forcing her to move
away from the machine. He starts to stitch, his foot pressing on
the pedal.*

PÈRE JULES: Have I ever seen a sewing machine!

JULIETTE *looks on amazed.* PÈRE JULES *beams triumphantly.*

JULIETTE: Well! You can do everything.
PÈRE JULES: I most certainly can. *(He looks at his hands)* What I
haven't used these for! *(Putting them round* JULIETTE'S *neck)*
One night in Shanghai, I even had to do this ... you give a good
squeeze ....

JULIETTE *pushes* PÈRE JULES *away to disengage herself; he
falls right off the bench, out of shot.*

JULIETTE: Now stop your nonsense, Père Jules.
PÈRE JULES: Stop pushing! I'm not a bad sort of chap, but if
someone provokes me ....

Full shot of PÈRE JULES *getting up.* JULIETTE *comes into shot
and snatches up the skirt which she has been stitching and which
is now lying on top of the sewing machine.*

JULIETTE: All right, Père Jules, as you're such a big shot, would
you mind putting on this skirt?

She hands him the skirt which he takes, bewildered.

PÈRE JULES: This skirt?
JULIETTE: Yes please. I want you to serve as dressmaker's
dummy so I can hem it.
PÈRE JULES: Oh. Yes. The hem, of course. But what am I meant
to do?

112

PÈRE JULES *clumsily slips on the skirt while* JULIETTE *goes to fetch some pins and a pair of scissors. Meanwhile,* PÈRE JULES *tries to look at himself with the skirt on and to button it round his waist.*

JULIETTE: Will you stop wriggling! Can't you button it up? Pull in your tummy!

She socks him in the stomach. He squeals, draws in his breath and can finally button up the skirt.

JULIETTE: What a lovely wasp waist you've got!

She pinches his waist, which makes him jump. The buttons come undone again. JULIETTE *kneels in front of him.*

PÈRE JULES: Don't tickle me!

PÈRE JULES *manages to do up the buttons again while* JULIETTE *starts to turn up the hem, kneeling in front of him with pins in her mouth.*

JULIETTE: Stop slouching. Hold yourself straight.
PÈRE JULES: No more tricks then, O.K?

He looks down at himself wearing the skirt and cannot resist dancing a little as he begins to sing.

PÈRE JULES: Travadja la Mouquère! Travadja Bono! *(whooping like an Indian)* Hou! Hou! Hou! Hou!

He dances about in the cabin. JULIETTE, *still on her knees, tries to follow him.*

PÈRE JULES, *still dancing and singing*: Hou! Hou! Hou!
JULIETTE: Stop it or I'll stick a pin into you!

She stabs him with one of her pins.

PÈRE JULES, *howling!*: Oula! Oulamaoula! Oula!
JULIETTE: You'd think you were still in darkest Africa.
PÈRE JULES: And that's not the only part of the world I know.

He raises his two index fingers and starts to do a Chinese dance.

PÈRE JULES, *singing*: Chin, chin, Chinaman, chop, chop, chop!

JULIETTE *tries to stab him again.* PÈRE JULES *now raises his fingers to his forehead and pretends to be a bull in a corrida.*

PÈRE JULES: Olé! Olé!

He begins to do a parody of a Spanish dance, stamping his feet and clicking his fingers, moving back all the time to stay out of JULIETTE'S *reach as she tries to stab him with her pin. He finally ends up squatting like a Russian moujik about to dance.*

PÈRE JULES, *singing and dancing*: Vo sadou li da vo grodie, Vyrasha Petrouchka, Maltchick dievotchkou selouiet, Doumaiet igrouchka.

JULIETTE *finally jumps up crossly.*

JULIETTE: Enough of that! You'll tear my skirt. Take it off.

She pulls the skirt off and it comes undone as it was only basted. PÈRE JULES *looks startled.*
JULIETTE *goes to pick up some clean laundry. She brings it back to* PÈRE JULES *who is now sitting down on the stool.*

JULIETTE: Be off with you! Here's your laundry.
PÈRE JULES: Give me time to catch my breath. I haven't done anything wrong. I'm exhausted.
JULIETTE: Are you going or aren't you?
PÈRE JULES: No, I'm not going. I won't, I won't, won't!

THE KID *comes in.*

THE KID: Père Jules .... We have to manoeuvre .... We're almost in Paris.

JULIETTE, *still holding her laundry, gapes at the news.*
PÈRE JULES *hurries out of the cabin. Fade in on the next shot.*
[*Long shot of the lock. All hands are on deck. Throughout this sequence, we hear the song of the Boatmen. We see* JEAN *and* JULIETTE *as l'Atalante rises in the lock.* JULIETTE, *still holding her bundle of clean laundry, gazes at the docks and the Ponte de Crimée as it opens to let them through.*]
Suddenly, JULIETTE *notices that she is clutching* PÈRE JULES'S *laundry and she goes into his cabin.*

JEAN, *at the helm, calls out to* PÈRE JULES.

JEAN: Père Jules, we're almost there. We're in sight of the docks of La Villette.

L'Atalante advances. PÈRE JULES *hurries up onto the deck without answering* JEAN. *We can see the docks in the background and hear the boat's siren.*

PÈRE JULES, *to* THE KID: I'll be up in a second. Get the boat ready for docking.

JULIETTE *has placed the clean laundry down on the bed in* PÈRE JULES'S *cabin. She has picked up a huge shell which she holds to her ear, trying to hear the sound of waves. We hear the boat siren announcing that l'Atalante is ready to dock.* PÈRE JULES *comes into the cabin and is a bit surprised to find* JULIETTE *there. She hands him the shell. He winds up a musical merry-go-round and shows it to her. She takes it and examines it while he puts the shell down on a special tray which plays a tune every time something is placed on it.* PÈRE JULES *picks the tray up to show* JULIETTE *how it works. Just then, an alarm clock starts to ting, mingling its sound with that of the two music-boxes.* PÈRE JULES *quickly leaves to stop the clock as* JULIETTE *looks on.*

PÈRE JULES *comes back into shot, still playing the musical merry-go-round. He is thoughtful, as though trying to remember something. He then goes off, once more, to another corner of the cabin.*

PÈRE JULES *is obviously searching for one object, displacing boxes, crates, etc. He finally produces an automat which holds a little baton like an orchestra conductor.* PÈRE JULES *blows the dust off the toy and starts to wind it up.*

JULIETTE *stops playing with the music box and turns to look at the automat with delight.*

The automat taps with its baton on a tiny music stand as though it were conducting.

* This sequence was never shot.

115

JULIETTE *begins to play the music box again. Music.*
The automat stops conducting and falls forward on the music
stand. PÈRE JULES *bows to the cats. The camera tracks to:*
JULIETTE, *looking round the cabin.*

JULIETTE: I didn't know you had all this in your cabin.
PÈRE JULES: Yes, it's a proper flea market I've got down here,
isn't it?
JULIETTE, *pointing to the gramophone*: What about this
gramophone?

PÈRE JULES: It doesn't work.

JULIETTE *looks at the various objects in the cabin, followed by*
PÈRE JULES. *She sees a large stiletto knife.*

JULIETTE: What a knife!
PÈRE JULES: It's called a *navaja,* and it's really sharp.

We hear the flick of the Spanish knife as PÈRE JULES *opens it.*
JULIETTE *still followed by* PÈRE JULES *is now peering into an*
old dresser. She takes out a framed photograph of a sailor.

JULIETTE: Is it you?

Shot of the photograph, held by JULIETTE.
JULIETTE, *looking at* PÈRE JULES *as she asks him the question.*

PÈRE JULES, *sadly*: That's a photo of my friend.

He puts the photograph back in its place. There is a brief but
awkward silence at this evocation of a dead friend. JULIETTE
looks away and sees a jar full of alcohol in which floats a human
hand.

PÈRE JULES: That's a lobster.

He scratches his chest and JULIETTE *sees something which*
draws her attention.

JULIETTE, *pointing to his chest*: What have you got there?
PÈRE JULES, *looking down*: What? My necklace?
JULIETTE, *pointing*: No. Those.
PÈRE JULES: Ah! My tattoos. You've never seen them before?

116

PÈRE JULES *proudly shows off his various tattoos to the startled* JULIETTE.

PÈRE JULES: You never feel the cold with those on you *(imitating the Parisian accent)*. Listen here, I'll play you a tune.

He picks up his accordion and starts to play it. Music. JULIETTE *takes a comb which is lying on a little shelf and starts to comb her hair. The accordion music stops.*

PÈRE JULES, *off*: You've got lovely hair, Missus.

JULIETTE *turns and the camera pans after her as she stretches out her arm to run the comb through* PÈRE JULES'S *hair.*

JULIETTE: So do you, Père Jules. Wait, I'll part your hair for you.
PÈRE JULES: Go ahead.

JULIETTE *starts combing* PÈRE JULES'S *hair.*

JEAN, *off*: What the hell is going on down there?

JULIETTE *and* PÈRE JULES *whirl round to look at:*
JEAN *coming down the cabin steps and walking up to where they stand.*

JEAN, *to* PÈRE JULES: What's all this? *(looking round).* What a mess there is in here. Fish nets everywhere. Eel pots. I've told you a hundred times that you're not supposed to have things like that on board *(turning on* JULIETTE*).* And what are you standing there for?

He suddenly catches sight of a photograph of a naked woman.

JEAN: And what about this photo?

Close up of the photograph. Then the camera tracks to:
PÈRE JULES, JEAN *and* JULIETTE.

PÈRE JULES: That's me when I was little.
JEAN: You when you were little? Are you trying to make a fool of me? And did you wear your hair like that when you were little too? What a hairdo! Just look at that mug!

PÈRE JULES *is uneasy. He would like to think of something clever to answer* JEAN. JULIETTE *is giggling nervously.*

Instinctively, PÈRE JULES *turns to look at himself in a mirror; he then turns to look daggers at* JULIETTE *who is still giggling.* JULIETTE *steps back and falls down on top of the laundry bundle which is lying on the bunk.*
Close up of PÈRE JULES *leaning over the still laughing* JULIETTE. *He stomps out of the cabin.*
JEAN *and* JULIETTE *remain alone in* PÈRE JULES'S *cabin.* JEAN *grabs* JULIETTE *by the wrist and roughly pulls her up from* PÈRE JULES'S *bunk. She pulls her wrist away and pushes* JEAN *back. Furious, he slaps her in the face. A moment later, realising what he is doing, he goes up to her, but she rebuffs his advances.* JEAN, *who is now angry with himself, begins to break some of the trinkets in the cabin.* JULIETTE, *horrified, cries out.*

JULIETTE: You're mad! Mad!

JEAN *stops, recovering his self-control.*

JULIETTE: You're not in your own place, you know.
JEAN, *losing his temper again*: Perhaps not, but you feel at home here, don't you?

We hear PÈRE JULES'S *footsteps as he comes down into the cabin. The young people turn to stare at him, for he has had all his hair shaved off.* PÈRE JULES *ignores them; he picks up a stool and sits down.*
On the quay, we see a dog barber sweeping up PÈRE JULES'S *hair and wiping his scissors.*
PÈRE JULES *sits motionless, his head completely shorn.* JEAN *and* JULIETTE *feel like laughing, but* JEAN *controls himself and leads* JULIETTE *out of the cabin.*
PÈRE JULES *still does not move. He then looks in the direction of his bunk and sits up.*

 *

Shot of the bundle of laundry which JULIETTE *has brought.* PÈRE JULES *picks it up, then hurls it down again angrily. He crumples one of his shirt collars and suddenly discovers a pair*

* Not shown in the final version.

118

of JULIETTE'S *panties which have been put inside his bundle by mistake. He cannot help laughing and leaves the cabin, holding the panties.*

JULIETTE *is alone in her cabin, sulking.* PÈRE JULES *comes in and, still laughing, hands her the panties. He slips out again, a smile on his lips.*

PÈRE JULES *meets* JEAN *on the deck just as* JEAN *is about to go on shore. Much to* JEAN'S *surprise,* PÈRE JULES *gives him a playful poke in the stomach.* PÈRE JULES *moves off, waving at* JEAN *in a friendly fashion. The dockers are busy unloading* l'Atalante.

JEAN, *a worried look on his face, reaches the headquarters of the Port Authorities. A bargee emerges from the building and, recognising* JEAN, *slaps him on the shoulder.*

THE BARGEE: Well, look who's here! How's your love life getting on?

JEAN: Pretty well.

THE BARGEE: I'll wait for you here.

JEAN: Fine. I'll just get these stamped. I'll only be a minute.

He goes into the headquarters of the Port Authorities.

Inside his cabin, PÈRE JULES *is good-humouredly inspecting the damage caused by* JEAN. *His expression changes when he sees the broken mirror lying on the floor.*

*

PÈRE JULES *picks up the pieces of mirror and, holding them in his hand, leaves the cabin. Just then, we hear* JEAN *calling his wife.*

JEAN, *off*: Juliette! Juliette!

Up on the deck, JEAN *is looking for* JULIETTE. PÈRE JULES *comes into shot, an anxious expression on his face.* THE KID *is already up on deck.*

* Not shown in the final version.

119

JEAN, *calling*: Juliette! Juliette! Where is she?
PÈRE JULES: She's down there.
JEAN: No, she's not. *(To a docker)* Have you seen her?

THE DOCKER *vaguely points his chin in the direction of the docks so that* JEAN, PÈRE JULES, *and* THE KID *all look that way.*

THE DOCKER: The missus? No, I haven't seen her.

JEAN *heads for his cabin.*

JEAN: Never mind. She'll turn up.

PÈRE JULES *looks down at his broken mirror and runs after* JEAN.
JEAN, PÈRE JULES, *soon followed by* THE KID.

PÈRE JULES: Maybe something's happened to her?

JEAN *walks forward and a ray of sunshine reflecting in the mirror catches his eye.* PÈRE JULES *also recalls the broken mirror and tosses it into the water.*

JEAN: What do you mean?
PÈRE JULES: You never know.

JEAN *and* THE KID *jump on shore in the wake of* PÈRE JULES. *The three of them agree to split up and set off in different directions to look for* JULIETTE.
PÈRE JULES, *looking for* JULIETTE *in one area of the docks.*
THE KID, *searching somewhere else.*
JEAN, *also looking for* JULIETTE; *he is soon joined by* PÈRE JULES *and* THE KID.
JEAN, PÈRE JULES *and* THE KID *all go back to l'Atalante which is still being unloaded. Suddenly, they see:*
JULIETTE *on a neighbouring barge, emerging from the cabin in the company of another woman.*

JULIETTE, *calling out to the three men*: So there you are! Where did you all disappear to?

She jumps onto the deck of l'Atalante and goes up to the three men. JEAN, PÈRE JULES *and* THE KID *look sheepish.*

Unperturbed, the dockers continue to unload their cargo.

JEAN: Oh, nowhere.
PÈRE JULES: We went strawberry-picking.

PÈRE JULES *and* THE KID *go down to their cabin,* JEAN *and* JULIETTE *to theirs.*

JEAN, *to the dockers*: Do you need me?
A DOCKER: What for?
JEAN: All right. How long will it take you to finish?
THE DOCKER: About an hour.

The dockers go on unloading.

L_____J

JEAN *and* JULIETTE *in their cabin.*

JULIETTE: Let's go out if they don't need you.
JEAN: We'd have to dress.
JULIETTE: I'd like to look around the city.
JEAN: That's true. All right, you get ready and I'll show you round.

JULIETTE *joyously starts to get ready.*
THE KID *is sweeping up inside* PÈRE JULES'S *cabin.* PÈRE JULES *scratches his neck and suddenly realises his good-luck pendant is missing.*

PÈRE JULES, *worriedly*: Have you seen my necklace?
THE KID: Your good-luck charm?

PÈRE JULES *feels inside his shirt and pulls out the broken necklace.*

PÈRE JULES: It's broken.

He looks down at the broken objects, including the fragments of mirror, which THE KID *has swept up in a heap.*

THE KID: You can repair it.
PÈRE JULES: It means a lot of bad luck to come. Let's go. And be quick about it.

He leaves, dragging THE KID *after him.*
JEAN *and* JULIETTE *inside their cabin; they are just about to go out.*

PÈRE JULES, *off*: Boss!
JULIETTE, *startled*: Oh! He scared me.
JEAN, *to* PÈRE JULES: What's the matter? Boat on fire?

He climbs up the cabin steps so that we soon see only his legs. PÈRE JULES *and* THE KID *are up on the deck.* JEAN *pokes his head out of the cabin hatch, close to their feet.*

PÈRE JULES: I'm going for a consultation.
JEAN: Are you ill?
PÈRE JULES: Not exactly, but I'm not exactly well either.

He goes off with THE KID, *and we see them leave the boat.* JEAN *comes back into the cabin, looking upset.*

JULIETTE, *happily*: Look! I'm ready.
JEAN: We've got to wait for Père Jules.
JULIETTE: Isn't he coming along too?
JEAN: No. He had to go off.
JULIETTE: Did he?
JEAN: Yes. He had to see the doctor because he's ill. He's taken the kid with him, so I can't leave the boat with no one on it.
JULIETTE: You might as well admit that we won't be going out after all.
JEAN: Of course we'll go out. But it'll have to be a bit later, that's all.

JULIETTE *begins to strip off her finery.*

JEAN: Don't get undressed!
JULIETTE: Why not? I don't need these to stay indoors. Your Père Jules won't turn up.

PÈRE JULES *and* THE KID *emerging from a bar. They start walking down a street, reach a small alleyway and stop.*
The camera follows PÈRE JULES *and* THE KID *as they enter a house in the alley.*
Inside the house, a dark staircase. PÈRE JULES *and* THE KID *are standing on a landing, ringing at a door. The door is opened*

122

by THE FORTUNE TELLER *they have come to see.* PÈRE JULES *and* THE KID *walk in, shutting the door behind them. The camera follows them into the room as* THE FORTUNE TELLER *leads them up to her table. She sits down.*
Shot of THE FORTUNE TELLER, *a plump woman with thick lips and glossy hair. She is wearing a great many rings and bracelets. She immediately goes into a kind of trance.*

THE FORTUNE TELLER: You two gentlemen are worried about something. You're worried and you wish to know if I can tell you about the future, which is neither wholly good nor wholly bad. *(She wakes up from her trance.)* Well, how do you want it? Divination? The tarot? Palmistry? Tea-leaves? The tables? Spiritualism? The crystal ball or the apparition of the devil? Do I handle both gentlemen at once? It'll cost you extra.

PÈRE JULES *and* THE KID.

PÈRE JULES: It's for me. My necklace broke.

He moves closer to THE FORTUNE TELLER.

THE FORTUNE TELLER: A necklace! What necklace? It sounds very serious.
PÈRE JULES: It is indeed.
THE FORTUNE TELLER: I'll use the cards. It'll cost you twenty francs. Sit down, please.

PÈRE JULES *sits down opposite* THE FORTUNE TELLER. THE KID *moves away and stands with his back to the wall.*
THE FORTUNE TELLER *and* PÈRE JULES.

PÈRE JULES: I'll be frank with you. Things aren't going too well on the boat.
THE FORTUNE TELLER, *as though inspired*: I can tell that Monsieur is a sailor.
PÈRE JULES: I was once. But today I want to find something out about a barge ....
THE FORTUNE TELLER: Cut the deck. Oh, what fantastic cards! All will be well, Sir. I see money and love, much love. Let me read your palm. What a love line! You're a greedy guts. A rover. Sensual. Devilish sensual. You must be a real lady-killer!

123

She lights a cigarette. PÈRE JULES *has begun to stare at her bosom and he starts getting familiar with her at these words.* PÈRE JULES *is now keenly interested in the person of* THE FORTUNE TELLER.

THE FORTUNE TELLER: Don't be worried. There is pleasure and happiness in store for you. That's all for now.

PÈRE JULES *and* THE FORTUNE TELLER *are flirting together while* THE KID *stands in his corner, uneasy at finding himself in this bizarre setting.*

THE FORTUNE TELLER: I will now tell you a great deal more.
PÈRE JULES: Will you?

They shoo away THE KID.

THE FORTUNE TELLER: Yes. In there.

We see a half-open door.
PÈRE JULES *and* THE FORTUNE TELLER *are now nudging each other playfully and giggling as they start going to the open door.*

PÈRE JULES: That's right. Tell me more. Much more!

They shut the door behind them; THE KID *remains alone in the room. He is scared.*

 *

Shot of the room.
Another corner of the room.

A ghost in a white sheet emerges from behind a curtain. It removes some of its coverings so that a bearded gentleman's head appears.

THE GHOST, *politely to* THE KID: Don't mind me. I'm the lady's husband.

* Shots never taken.

The ghost then takes a cigarette and a newspaper from the table, nods to THE KID *and vanishes behind the curtain again. Tracking shot of* THE GHOST.

THE FORTUNE TELLER *and* PÈRE JULES, *both looking very pleased with themselves.*

THE FORTUNE TELLER: There, you see? You'll be happy for the rest of your life. Come and see me again. Ten francs, plus twenty francs. You owe me thirty francs.

 *

PÈRE JULES *puts the money down on the table.*

PÈRE JULES: Your cards are always right, aren't they? I can be quite sure that things will turn out all right for everyone on l'Atalante, like you said?

THE FORTUNE TELLER *picks up a publicity card from her table.*

THE FORTUNE TELLER: Can't you read? It says: Madame Clara is one of the top voyantes in the business. Here it is in print.

PÈRE JULES *takes the card, then gives it back to* THE FORTUNE TELLER.

PÈRE JULES: Sorry.

THE FORTUNE TELLER *presses a handful of these cards on* PÈRE JULES *who tries to refuse.*

THE FORTUNE TELLER: Go ahead. Take them. Stop fussing. Here's some to give to your friends.

They walk up to the front door. Before following them out, THE KID *goes past the table and picks up the thirty francs left there by* PÈRE JULES.

THE FORTUNE TELLER: See you again soon.
PÈRE JULES: So long.

PÈRE JULES *and* THE KID *leave the flat.* THE FORTUNE

* Not included in the final version.

TELLER *shuts the door after them and then rests against the door for a moment, closing her eyes and smiling.*
We see first PÈRE JULES, *then* THE KID, *as they come out into the street.* PÈRE JULES *puts out his hand and* THE KID *gives him back the thirty francs. They go off together.*

JEAN *is looking out for* PÈRE JULES *on the deck of l'Atalante.*
JULIETTE'S *head emerges out of the cabin hatch.*

JULIETTE: How much longer are you going to wait up for your Père Jules?
JEAN: He'll be back any minute.
JULIETTE: I don't feel like going out now, anyway.

She goes back into the cabin where JEAN *follows her.*
It is dusk now and the street-lamps are already lit. So are the lights in the bar in front of which PÈRE JULES *and* THE KID *are standing.*

PÈRE JULES: Go home. You ought to be in bed.

THE KID *obeys him and leaves.*

PÈRE JULES: Well, I don't have to worry any more. The cards are on my side.

He marches into the bar.
JEAN *and* JULIETTE *are sitting on their bed inside the cabin, still waiting for* PÈRE JULES. *Suddenly, they hear the sound of footsteps on the deck.* JEAN *rushes out of the cabin.*

JEAN: Père Jules!
THE KID, *off*: He's busy. He'll be back later.

JEAN *climbs down again.* JULIETTE *prepares the bed for the night.*

JULIETTE: I knew it.

It is night. A drunkard staggers along the river's edge. He seems about to fall in at every step.
PÈRE JULES *is watching the drunkard admiringly.*

PÈRE JULES: Carry on, old chap, you're doing really well. Bravo!

The drunkard totters up to the spot where PÈRE JULES *is standing and applauding his performance. He bows to* PÈRE JULES *and keels over in the process.* PÈRE JULES *helps him back on his feet.*

PÈRE JULES: Monsieur has had a drop to drink?

The drunkard bows again and leaves. He almost falls into the river and PÈRE JULES *grabs him just in time, propping him up against a tree. The drunkard is about to collapse once more:* PÈRE JULES *begins to slap him to make him stay up.*

PÈRE JULES: Mind your manners! Stay right there, I'll be back tomorrow morning.

He walks away.
PÈRE JULES *walks past a tramp who is lying under a bridge. The tramp sleeps surrounded by bits and pieces, among them an old gramophone case which attracts* PÈRE JULES'S *attention.* PÈRE JULES *grabs the case and puts his head inside it.*

PÈRE JULES, *shouting* : Anyone at home?

The tramp wakes up with a start.

THE TRAMP: Oh, it's you, is it?
PÈRE JULES: Will you sell me this?
THE TRAMP: You can have it. It's a gift.

PÈRE JULES *goes off with the gramophone case.* THE TRAMP *falls asleep again and begins to snore loudly.*

---

* Not shown in the final version.

It is night now. JULIETTE *is up on the deck, looking in the direction of the city.*

PÈRE JULES, *loudly singing off*: Paris, O city of sin and delight, Beloved by lovers and thieves, You bewitch everyone with your light ... etc.

JULIETTE *goes down to her cabin.*
Inside the cabin, JULIETTE *takes her coat off and slips into bed next to the sleeping* JEAN. *He wakes up and takes her in his arms.*

JEAN: Oh! There you are! You're not asleep? I dreamt you were leaving me. What a nightmare.

She kisses him. We hear loud knocking on the cabin door. It is PÈRE JULES *who is completely drunk.*

PÈRE JULES, *off:* Whatsa matter? Do I have to go and call the Police? Wake up, willya!

JEAN *looks at* JULIETTE, *then jumps up and goes to the door.*

JEAN: It's Père Jules.

JEAN, *in his nightshirt, goes up the cabin steps, opens the hatch and sees* PÈRE JULES *who is singing at the top of his voice, his head still inside the gramophone case.*

PÈRE JULES: Paris, O city of sin and delight, Paris, etc. ....

PÈRE JULES *stumbles down into the cabin and falls over, dead drunk.* JEAN *and* JULIETTE *push him back up onto the deck.*

 *

JEAN *comes back into the cabin and goes over to the chair on which his clothes are lying. He starts pulling on his trousers.* JULIETTE *watches him, worried. We can still hear* PÈRE JULES *singing lustily.*

JEAN: Just you wait. I'll give you a Paris ....

* Not included in the final version.

He leaves the cabin. JULIETTE *remains alone, listening anxiously to what is going on up on deck.* PÈRE JULES *is belting out his song. He stops abruptly when the gramophone case is knocked off his head and crashes down onto the deck.*

PÈRE JULES, *off*: Don't touch me I tell you! Stoppit!

JEAN *and* PÈRE JULES *up on the deck of l'Atalante. It is night.* PÈRE JULES *is picking up the gramophone case.*

PÈRE JULES: So I ain't even got the right to sing anymore. Then who's going to sing in my place, eh?
JEAN: If you don't like it, you can just pack your bags and leave.
PÈRE JULES: My bags? Yeah, I'll pack 'em. I'm going, but I'm not going alone. You're leaving with me, feet first. D'you hear me? You're leaving this barge too, feet first!

PÈRE JULES *goes down into his cabin.*
Inside his cabin, PÈRE JULES *is loading an enormous revolver. He notices that* THE KID'S *blanket has slipped off the bed and shoves the revolver in his pocket to rearrange the bed. He then leaves the cabin, growling threats.*

PÈRE JULES: I've never missed a single one. Pity it always has to end this way.

Inside the other cabin, JULIETTE *is getting out of bed. On hearing the loud sound of a pistol going off, she freezes, then rushes over to the staircase.*
It is night. Up on the deck, alone, PÈRE JULES *gazes down at a bullet hole in his trousers near his knee. The gun has gone off accidentally in his pocket. He takes the smoking revolver out of his pocket.*

PÈRE JULES: Let all men take warning.

JEAN *comes into shot, soon followed by* JULIETTE *in her nightgown.*

JEAN: You idiot! You could have hurt yourself. How clumsy can you get, letting a gun go off all by itself inside your pocket! Here, give it to me. When a chap can't handle these things they're better off in the water.

The embarrassed PÈRE JULES *is still holding the revolver.* JEAN *takes it from him and tosses it into the water.*

PÈRE JULES: It'll get rusty.
JEAN: I'll make you even rustier. Go to bed.

⎣▁▁▁▁▁▁▁▁▁▁▁▁▁▁▁▁▁▁▁▁▁⎦

He drags PÈRE JULES *away. As they go,* PÈRE JULES *notices that* JULIETTE *is wearing only her nightgown. He begins to laugh.*

PÈRE JULES: Look at the missus in her nightie!

JULIETTE *slips away.*

PÈRE JULES, *singing:* Paris, Paris, oh city of sin and delight, etc.

JEAN *drags* PÈRE JULES *down the stairs.* THE KID *gets up and* JULIETTE *comes back, wearing a coat. The three of them put* PÈRE JULES *to bed.*

JEAN: Every time we get to a city he acts like this. The less time we spend in a town the better. We're all awake, so we might as well leave now. You two can help me get the boat started.

JEAN, JULIETTE *and* THE KID *go off, leaving* PÈRE JULES *on his own. The sound of the ticking clock is drowned by the sound of the boat engines starting up.*
JEAN *and* JULIETTE *are up on deck. It is night and the barge is slowly moving out of the docks.*
L'Atalante *chugs away in the night. We can see the lights of Paris receding.*
We return to JEAN *and* JULIETTE *sitting together.*

JEAN: You're not cross with me, are you?
JULIETTE: No. Why should I be?
JEAN: It was hard luck on you. For once that we were in Paris and Père Jules spoiled everything.
JULIETTE: It's not the first time.
JEAN: We'll be back, and I promise you we'll have a lot of fun. There's so much to see. I'll take you up the Eiffel Tower. 300 metres above sea-level.

130

JULIETTE: Go on, you're just saying that.
JEAN: You don't believe me? For a start, we'll go someplace tomorrow before we're even as far as Corbeil.
JEAN: You promise?
JEAN: I promise. It's as good as done.

A restaurant-cum-dancehall. The sign reads 'Aux Nations.' JEAN *and* JULIETTE *are walking towards it, looking pleased and happy. The camera tracks to a* TRAVELLING SALESMAN *who is riding a bicycle at breakneck speed down a hill, in the direction of* JEAN *and* JULIETTE. *We hear the loud tinkle of his bicycle bell.*
Startled by the bicycle bell, JEAN *and* JULIETTE *jump out of* THE SALESMAN'S *way.*
Shot of THE SALESMAN, *astride his bicycle, carrying a suitcase strapped to his back. On the suitcase, we see lettering: 'The goodies are in here.'* THE SALESMAN *stops and starts pedalling backwards so as to speak to the young couple whom he has almost knocked over.*
THE SALESMAN *moves closer to* JEAN *and* JULIETTE *who haven't the heart to get angry with him.*

THE SALESMAN: Good day to you, Madam, and to you, Sir. Beg pardon if I startled you. No hard feelings, I hope. Let me introduce myself; me name is Jean-Louis-Paul-Aimé-Désiré-Dupont, in other words the king of travelling salesmen, that's a fact.

He cycles off again, doffing his hat to them; just as he is vanishing from sight, we see his suitcase burst open. JEAN *and* JULIETTE *start walking towards their destination once again.*

THE SALESMAN, *from afar*: Bidibing, tsouin tsouin! So long! Cheerio! Pip pip!

JEAN and JULIETTE *reach the restaurant-dancehall and the first thing they see is* THE TRAVELLING SALESMAN'S *bicycle propped up next to the entrance. They walk into the dance-hall. Inside the restaurant, the orchestra is playing full-swing and couples are dancing on the floor in the middle of the tables where other couples sit. The music stops and the dancing*

131

couples go back to their places. As the dance-floor empties, we can see THE TRAVELLING SALESMAN *already busy turning himself into the centre of attention and in the act of starting up his spiel. He catches sight of* JEAN *and* JULIETTE *when they come in and rushes up to greet them.*

JEAN *and* JULIETTE *stand near the door.* THE TRAVELLING SALESMAN *comes into shot and starts leading them up to a table, going into an act as he does so.*

THE TRAVELLING SALESMAN: My dear friends, Madam, Sir, how very kind of you to come. We were waiting for you before we started the ball rolling, rolling ball, roly poly, Polly put the kettle on, ha, ha!

Insert of the restaurant proprietor looking on somewhat anxiously.

THE TRAVELLING SALESMAN *whisks* JEAN'S *cap off his head and a bird flies out from underneath it.*

THE TRAVELLING SALESMAN: Dear me, Sir, you've brought a birdie with you.

He pulls a dress out of JEAN'S *pocket.*

THE TRAVELLING SALESMAN: Thank you kindly *(to* JULIETTE*).* Pretty dress that, Madam. How do you like this handkerchief? Won't shrink, won't tear, won't leak, won't bend … *(taking out a pack of cards)* take a card, any card. Ten of spades? Certainly. Here it is, our pretty little ten of spades!

The ten of spades seems to leap out of the deck. THE TRAVELLING SALESMAN *then starts pulling more cards from under the nose of another man.*

THE TRAVELLING SALESMAN *to the man*: You thief you!

JEAN *and* JULIETTE *look on,* JEAN *somewhat irritated,* JULIETTE *delighted.* THE TRAVELLING SALESMAN *goes back to the centre of the dance floor. His case springs open and the merchandise spills out all over the floor as people jostle around him. The restaurant proprietor rushes over, alarmed at the turmoil which is being caused in his establishment.*

THE TRAVELLING SALESMAN *picks up a guitar and starts singing to draw everyone's attention and to make them draw closer and buy his merchandise.*

THE TRAVELLING SALESMAN, *singing*:

> I am a Paris drummer,
> I sell beneath the Paris skies.
> The Paris skies are pigeon grey,
> they make ladies look so gay.
> Oh those café terraces,
> there are so many, you can't count 'em,
> and that's where the action is!
> Look at all my lovely wares,
> I don't sell elephants or bears,
> Only goodies, only prizes,
> and surprises!
>
> Just take a look at my things,
> a look won't cost you anything.
> Just think of tomorrow, my oh my,
> When you're lying in bed
> And you're feeling so sad,
> 'Cos you didn't buy.
> I bring luck and I bring joy,
> I am not fly, I am not coy.
> I'm just telling you in all honesty
> That these knives, these shiny knives
> Will not rust while you're alive.
>
> The country's nothing like the city,
> They're so different that it's a pity.
> Here, my little chickadee,
> Smell this perfume from Paree.
> I sell lace to all the ladies,
> I sell combs to all the laddies.
> Each offer extra special, you bet,

* Not included in the final version.

133

At the lowest prices yet.
The latest, the sharpest,
The finest, oh yes!

You'll find it all right here,
Brushes and all the gear.
You'll get an honest deal,
These satin bows are real.
Toys for the kiddies,
Toothpicks and wigs for grannies.
Ladies and gentlemen, stop right here,
My merchandise ain't dear.
etc. ... etc. ...

THE TRAVELLING SALESMAN *dances about the room as he
sings his song.*
He goes and sits with JEAN *and* JULIETTE, *still singing his song.
When* JULIETTE *looks away, he calls out 'Coucou!'*

THE TRAVELLING SALESMAN: You're pretty. *(He looks at*
JEAN*)* You're pretty too, but your wife's even prettier!

He leaves them.
THE TRAVELLING SALESMAN *is taking out his merchandise,
showing off various items and scattering them about the room.*

THE TRAVELLING SALESMAN, *calling out*: Coucou! Coucou!

He begins his spiel and the music starts up again.
THE TRAVELLING SALESMAN *performs a trick with a thimble,
then another trick with a loaded dice, then he makes a scarf
disappear.*
He fits up an old sailor with a pair of spectacles.

THE TRAVELLING SALESMAN: I can see that Monsieur needs
glasses just by the naughty gleam in his eye! Beautiful. May I take
your picture, sir? *(He takes a picture)*. Thank you. That'll be ten
francs for the glasses and as I'm an honest sort of chap I'll tell you
a secret: there's no film in my camera.

The band gaily plays some dance music.

134

Long shot of the restaurant. THE TRAVELLING SALESMAN'S *merchandise is scattered all over the dance-floor and is getting in the way of the dancers.*
The proprietor looks on.

THE PROPRIETOR: He's going too far.

The waiters and THE PROPRIETOR *grab* THE TRAVELLING SALESMAN *and his merchandise, dragging him off the dance floor so that the clients can dance.* THE TRAVELLING SALESMAN, *firmly held by the collar, does the split, pretending to slip about the floor as he is led away.*
JULIETTE *is looking on, amused.*
THE TRAVELLING SALESMAN, *now relegated to a dark corner of the room, waves to* JULIETTE *with a glove puppet, over the heads of the dancers.*
JULIETTE *laughs;* JEAN *looks grim.*
THE TRAVELLING SALESMAN *jumps up from his table and goes over to where the young couple sits, jostling past groups of dancers.* JEAN *buys a scarf from him in the hope that this will make him go away. But* THE TRAVELLING SALESMAN *grabs* JULIETTE *just as* JEAN *is about to pay for the scarf.*

THE TRAVELLING SALESMAN: I'll throw this dance in for free as a bonus to the lady who's bought one of my scarves!

JEAN *looks on bleakly as* THE TRAVELLING SALESMAN *whisks* JULIETTE *onto the dance-floor.*
THE TRAVELLING SALESMAN *and* JULIETTE, *dancing.*

THE TRAVELLING SALESMAN: So you've never been to Paris?
JULIETTE: I've never been to any big city.
THE TRAVELLING SALESMAN: You don't say? Is it a fact? Ah, Paris! What a city! Nothing like it in the world. It's fantastic. If only I could show you around, you'd learn a trick or too, you would.

JEAN *is visibly irritated.* THE TRAVELLING SALESMAN *and* JULIETTE *dance past him.*
Shot of THE TRAVELLING SALESMAN *and* JULIETTE *dancing together.*
Shot of JEAN. THE TRAVELLING SALESMAN *dances past him*

135

again. *Suddenly,* JEAN *jumps up and pushes* THE TRAVELLING SALESMAN *out of the way, throwing the scarf down and dragging his wife out of the dance hall.* THE TRAVELLING SALESMAN, *trying to be clever, dashes after them and tries to thrust the scarf on them.*

THE TRAVELLING SALESMAN: If the lady belongs to you, so does the scarf! You paid for it, Mister. Cash ....

JEAN *whirls round and knocks down* THE TRAVELLING SALESMAN. *He then leaves the dance hall with* JULIETTE. *The band stops as* THE TRAVELLING SALESMAN *lands headlong on the floor and people mill about to see what is happening.*
JEAN *and* JULIETTE, *seen through the plate glass window of a bar: they are walking along the quays, arguing and gesticulating wildly.*
The restaurant PROPRIETOR *now turns wrathfully on the poor* TRAVELLING SALESMAN.

THE PROPRIETOR: I won't put up with this sort of behaviour! Clear off, and don't ever let me catch sight of you again.

┌─────────────────────┐ *

THE TRAVELLING SALESMAN *peeking through a window. The furious* PROPRIETOR *catches sight of him and* THE TRAVELLING SALESMAN *makes himself scarce.*
A bizarrely dressed man comes into the restaurant by another door. Everyone, including THE PROPRIETOR, *gapes at the odd figure in astonishment. The stranger takes his hat off and we recognise* THE TRAVELLING SALESMAN *who quickly runs off again.*
THE TRAVELLING SALESMAN, *still wearing his odd disguise, is trotting down a quay. We can see* JEAN *and* JULIETTE *walking in the distance. The camera tracks to:*
JEAN *and* JULIETTE. THE TRAVELLING SALESMAN, *in his disguise, catches up with them and finally turns down a sideroad.*

JEAN: I've had just about enough!

* Not included in the final version.

136

JULIETTE: We weren't doing anything wrong. He was telling me about Paris and I was saying that you had promised to take me there on a visit.

JEAN: Enough of that. And as for taking you into town, we'll see about that another time.

Insert of THE TRAVELLING SALESMAN *going off on his bicycle.* JEAN *and* JULIETTE *have reached l'Atalante.*
A knife is being hurled through the air; its blade point lands in the wooden wall of PÈRE JULES'S *cabin.* THE KID *comes into shot, pulls out the knife and goes back to the spot where* PÈRE JULES *is standing.*

PÈRE JULES: Your turn.

THE KID *throws the knife and misses the target. He fetches the knife which* PÈRE JULES *takes from him.*

PÈRE JULES: Missed again! You'll never know how to fight for your life at the speed you're learning. Come on, give it here. Where do you want me to throw it next? Over there?

He throws a knife at a target off screen.
Shot of the knife where it has landed: straight between the eyes of a hat-stand dummy.

━━━━━━━━━━━━━━━━━━

JEAN *and* JULIETTE, *inside their cabin.*

JEAN: At least you can't get into trouble here.
JULIETTE: Are you going somewhere?
JEAN: Yes.
JULIETTE: Aren't you taking me with you?
JEAN: No.

He leaves with PÈRE JULES.
THE TRAVELLING SALESMAN'S *head appears above the wall. He is obviously on the lookout for something or someone.*
Shot of JEAN, PÈRE JULES *and* THE KID *as they walk away rapidly along the towpath.*
JEAN, PÈRE JULES *and* THE KID *disappear down a side-turning.*

137

The coast is clear. THE TRAVELLING SALESMAN *slips into the open, carrying various musical instruments. He starts to play as he walks.*
Inside the cabin, JULIETTE *hears the music and goes up on deck.*
On deck, JULIETTE'S *head appears out of the hatch close to the legs of* THE TRAVELLING SALESMAN *who goes on serenading her.*

JULIETTE: What are you doing here? What about my husband?
THE TRAVELLING SALESMAN: Your husband is a civilised man, my dear.
JULIETTE: Aren't you frightened?
THE TRAVELLING SALESMAN: They say that music soothes the nerves. Please, Madam, I beg you not to remain lying at my feet.

> JULIETTE *comes out onto the deck.*
> JEAN, *walking with* PÈRE JULES *and* THE KID, *suddenly stops in his tracks and starts to look for something which he has obviously left behind.*

JEAN: Wait for me, I'll be back right away.

> *He turns and starts walking back towards l'Atalante with a rapid stride.* PÈRE JULES *and* THE KID *hesitate a little, then begin to follow* JEAN *from a distance.*
> THE TRAVELLING SALESMAN *and* JULIETTE.

THE TRAVELLING SALESMAN: I came to apologise and to give you a musical farewell. Here's your scarf. You forgot it.
JULIETTE: Oh! Thank you.
THE TRAVELLING SALESMAN: It comes from Paris. Best quality. Latest fashion. A souvenir from the big city, you might say. I'll be in Paris myself this very evening (*jokingly*). Why don't you come with me? I'll take you for a quick spin. Is it a deal?

> *Shot of* JULIETTE.
> THE TRAVELLING SALESMAN, *then* JULIETTE.

THE TRAVELLING SALESMAN: You want to have a bit of fun, don't you? You'll only end up with rheumatism on this old craft. I'll take you on my bike. You'll be back before curfew. Is it a deal? Paris ... the city of light! Lights everywhere. And the elegance! And the motorcycles, the cars! Beautiful! Ah, the Champs Elysées! Or if you prefer, Notre Dame! The Eiffel Tower, if that's what you've set your heart on.

THE TRAVELLING SALESMAN *keeps on hopping from the deck of l'Atalante to the towpath and back again onto the deck.* JULIETTE *watches him, amused.*

THE TRAVELLING SALESMAN: Do I hear an offer? Shall I wrap it up? Is it a deal? Going, going, gone!

He moves off. JULIETTE *looks at him, still amused; then her expression changes to one of dismay.*

THE TRAVELLING SALESMAN: Do I hear an offer?

THE TRAVELLING SALESMAN. JEAN *comes up behind him and kicks him on the backside.* THE TRAVELLING SALESMAN *is frightened, yet automatically cracks a joke as* JULIETTE *comes into shot.*

THE TRAVELLING SALESMAN: Did I hear someone knock?

JEAN *pushes him roughly off the boat.* JULIETTE *looks on.* THE TRAVELLING SALESMAN *lands on the towpath.*

THE TRAVELLING SALESMAN: I'll take my leave now. Bunch of dummies!

He runs off.

┌──────────────────────┐ *

PÈRE JULES *and* THE KID *close to a house painter perched on a ladder.* PÈRE JULES *overhears* THE TRAVELLING SALESMAN'S *parting words.*

PÈRE JULES: Bunch of dummies? I'll show you who's the dummy!

He dashes forward with THE KID *to grab* THE TRAVELLING SALESMAN. *He tries, in vain, to stop* THE KID *from running underneath the ladder.*

* Not included in the final version.

PÈRE JULES: Don't go under the ladder!

Shot of the house painter standing on one of the upper rungs of the ladder. The bucket of paint topples over.
THE KID, *with his head under the paint bucket.*
PÈRE JULES *in despair.*

PÈRE JULES: What next? First a broken mirror and now a ladder. We're really in luck.

The cabin. JULIETTE *is lying in bed, wide awake. We can hear* JEAN *pacing up and down on the deck above.* JULIETTE *catches sight of the scarf lying on a chair.*

THE TRAVELLING SALESMAN'S Voice: Comes from Paris. Highest quality. Latest fashion. A souvenir of the big city, you might say.
JEAN'S Voice: Why did you stay on the deck? He was chatting you up. You were all ears. Paris! The big city! I'll make sure you don't go anywhere near there for quite a while.
THE TRAVELLING SALESMAN'S Voice: I'll be in Paris this evening. Why don't you come with me for a quick spin? It's a deal!

Shot of JEAN *pacing up and down the deck. Night.*

THE TRAVELLING SALESMAN'S Voice: Going, going, gone! I'll take you with me without so much as a by-your-leave.

JULIETTE *lying in bed, still alone and still wide-awake.* JEAN *comes in and starts to take his jacket off.* JULIETTE *turns her back to him. Furious, he pulls on his jacket again and leaves the cabin.* JULIETTE *gets up.*
Inside PÈRE JULES'S *cabin.* THE KID *is asleep.* PÈRE JULES *is holding a pack of cards. He draws a card: it is the ten of spades. He takes out another card: it is the ace of spades.*

PÈRE JULES: Another spade. And in the middle of the night too!

He takes a swig of rum.
JULIETTE *slips off the boat and disappears into the night.*

Insert: JEAN *changes his mind and decides to walk back towards the boat.*
JEAN *walking back along the towpath.*
JULIETTE *climbing into a tram. Night.*
JEAN *in the empty cabin.* JULIETTE *is gone. He opens the closet, sees that she has taken her coat and leaves the cabin again.*
JULIETTE *inside the tram as it clatters down a road at night.*
JEAN *inside* PÈRE JULES'S *cabin.*

JEAN: We're leaving, I tell you.
PÈRE JULES: But we were supposed to remain here another two days ....
JEAN: That's my business. I don't want your advice. Did I ask you for it yesterday evening at La Villette?
PÈRE JULES: Maybe you didn't, boss, but that's got nothing to do with it. I've got the right to not be asleep right now, but that doesn't mean I have to work every night I choose to go to bed late. I'm not doing anything wrong, am I?
JEAN: It has nothing to do with you.
PÈRE JULES: Then what's the matter?
JEAN: It's the missus. She's gone.
PÈRE JULES: Gone? But where?
JEAN: I don't want to know. I'd rather we left.
PÈRE JULES: Wait a minute! She'll be back any minute now. Or maybe in an hour's time. Or else tomorrow at the latest.
JEAN: Tomorrow! I wouldn't take her back if she returned in five minutes' time.
PÈRE JULES: Maybe so, but that doesn't mean we can't get any rest. We said we'd leave in two days' time, so let's stay here for another day and go and look for the missus tomorrow.
JEAN: Go look for her? What for, you idiot? Listen, I'm the boss of this ship and I want both you and the boy to come up on deck right away.

Dawn. JULIETTE *gets off the tram. We see her looking into shop windows at clothes and jewellery.*
L'Atalante, going full steam.
JULIETTE *in the big city.*
L'Atalante, going full speed.

141

JULIETTE *returning down the towpath.*
JULIETTE *standing next to the spot where l'Atalante was moored.*
The deserted canal.
Empty, canvas-covered barges.

```
┌──────────────────────────┐  *
```

A cat comes into shot and follows JULIETTE.
JULIETTE *and the cat walking off together.*
Long shot of the canal.
A man comes running towards JULIETTE. *She dashes off.*
JULIETTE *escaping.*
JULIETTE *running away.*
L'Atalante going full speed.

```
└──────────────────────────┘
```

JULIETTE *reaching the town.*
She comes to a railway station.
The ticket seller's window. JULIETTE *asks for a third class ticket to Corbeil.*
JULIETTE *opens her handbag.*
A man rushes past JULIETTE, *grabs her handbag and runs off.*

JULIETTE: Stop! Thief!

JULIETTE *and others running after the thief.*

PEOPLE: Stop him! Thief! Murder! Help!

The man disappears in the street.
JULIETTE *looks hopeless.*
L'Atalante moves further away.
Tracking shot of thief, passer-by, JULIETTE, *a lady and a gentleman walking in the opposite direction.*
JULIETTE *disappears amid the crowd and the traffic.*
Succession of shots: JULIETTE *looking for work. A factory with men queuing in front of entrance. A placard with the words 'NO VACANCIES' printed on it. Another factory with a*

---

* Not included in the final version.

similar queue of men. Men calling out to JULIETTE.

JULIETTE *ends up in front of a boatsmen's café. She goes up to the door but cannot bring herself to go in. She walks past the café two or three times, peers in and finally makes up her mind to enter.*

Inside PÈRE JULES'S *cabin* PÈRE JULES *and* JEAN *are playing a game of checkers.* THE KID *looks on, a cat lying on his lap.*

PÈRE JULES: Come on, boss, it's your turn.

JEAN *is in a torpor. A hand comes into shot and pushes a piece across the board. The piece is taken.*
Camera pans so that we see it is PÈRE JULES *who is pushing the piece and playing in* JEAN'S *place.*

PÈRE JULES: Well done! My turn now *(taking several pieces at a time)* One, two, three, four and a queen. Your turn, boss, *(he plays for* JEAN*)* Not bad. My turn now. Even better. Your turn.

JEAN *wakes out of his trance and plays, taking three pieces.*

PÈRE JULES: Oh ho! Cheating now? Well, never mind.

JEAN *sinks back into his lethargy.*
PÈRE JULES *takes advantage of* JEAN'S *absent-mindedness to turn the board around, giving his pieces to* JEAN *and taking* JEAN'S, *which are in a better position.*

PÈRE JULES: My turn.

He pushes a piece. JEAN *pushes another and is about to win.*
PÈRE JULES *looks annoyed and crossly taps the edge of the board. He winks in* THE KID'S *direction.*
THE KID *brushes the cat off his lap.*
The cat knocks the board over.

PÈRE JULES: Oh damn! We can't continue this game. And just when I was about to win too!

JEAN *goes over to a bucket full of water and plunges his head inside it. He then leaves the cabin.*
PÈRE JULES *is left alone with* THE KID.

PÈRE JULES: You see? He's at it again. He's off his rocker *(picking up his record and pointing to the phonograph)*. If only we

143

could play this. It might take his mind off his problems. I've been working on that phonograph for six months and yesterday I thought I'd made a breakthrough. Oh well ....

As he talks he pensively runs his finger round the record and we suddenly hear the sound of accordion music. Startled, PÈRE JULES stops running his finger round the record. The music stops too. He starts again and so does the music. PÈRE JULES stares at his finger and is about to try again when he hears THE KID giggling.
Shot of THE KID grinning and holding the accordion.
Shot of PÈRE JULES, furious.

PÈRE JULES: Go ahead! Laugh! Stranger things have happened than that. Electricity, for example. What do you know about electricity?

He winds up the phonograph and puts on the record. It does not work.

PÈRE JULES *furious*: Take that!

He hits the gramophone, which instantly starts to play. THE KID comes closer and they both listen to the music. PÈRE JULES looks in the direction of the accordion.

PÈRE JULES, *delighted*: This time it's not a trick. It really works. Go fetch the boss.

THE KID rushes up the cabin steps and looks out on the deck. JEAN, wild-eyed, is in the act of throwing himself into the river, fully dressed.
THE KID at the top of the cabin steps.

THE KID, *shouting*: Père Jules! The boss has just thrown himself into the water!

PÈRE JULES rushes forwards towards THE KID and they both leave the cabin.
Underwater shot of JEAN swimming below the surface.
Close up of JEAN. His eyes are wide open.
JEAN in the water. Superimposition of JULIETTE smiling, wearing her wedding dress.

JEAN *in the water. Apparition of* JULIETTE.

PÈRE JULES *and* THE KID *looking anxiously down into the water.*

JEAN *emerging from the water from the opposite side of the barge and going up to* PÈRE JULES *and* THE KID *from behind. He looks over their shoulders to stare at the water too.* PÈRE JULES *catches sight of him and hastily leads him down into the cabin.*

PÈRE JULES: Now boss, what's come over you? You'll catch pneumonia. Hurry up and change your clothes.

Inside PÈRE JULES'S *cabin. The cats are grouped around the gramophone.*

PÈRE JULES *and* THE KID *help* JEAN *out of his wet clothing.* JEAN *remains silent and* PÈRE JULES *speaks for him as well as for himself.*

PÈRE JULES: What did you say? You were going fishing, was that it? I thought that was what you said.

PÈRE JULES *finishes dressing* JEAN, *who still does not react.* PÈRE JULES *tickles him.*

PÈRE JULES: Kiri-Kiki!

Not knowing how to shake JEAN *out of his torpor* PÈRE JULES *suddenly cries out to* THE KID:

PÈRE JULES: My gramophone! Go fetch the orchestra.

THE KID *rushes out of the cabin.* PÈRE JULES *and* JEAN *remain alone.*

PÈRE JULES: Boss, I'm going to show you my latest invention!

He drags JEAN *off with him.*
On the deck. THE KID *comes out of* PÈRE JULES'S *cabin, carrying the gramophone.* PÈRE JULES *and* JEAN *arrive,* PÈRE JULES *leading* JEAN *by the hand.* PÈRE JULES *makes* JEAN *sit down and gestures to the kid.* THE KID *starts putting on the record.*

PÈRE JULES: No, the other side. It's more lively.

He suddenly has an idea and drags THE KID *off to his cabin.*
Music. The gramophone. Pan to JEAN *who sits dreaming. We*
hear PÈRE JULES *and* THE KID *giving great whoops.*
PÈRE JULES *and* THE KID *wearing fancy dress begin to dance.*
Music.
They dance. JEAN, *in the background, is the only one of the*
three who is not enjoying himself.
JEAN *in the foreground.* PÈRE JULES *and* THE KID *having a*
great time. Suddenly, JEAN *gets up and leaves.*
PÈRE JULES *and* THE KID *are rolling about with laughter.*
JEAN *moves off.* PÈRE JULES *and* THE KID *notice his chair is*
empty. They stop laughing. Their plan to amuse JEAN *has*
failed.
JEAN *looking at the river bank.*
JULIETTE *walking down a wharf.*
The barge moving on the water. JEAN *staring at the bank as the*
boat passes.
JULIETTE *watching barges move on the water.*
JEAN *going to his cabin.*
JULIETTE *walking towards a ferry.*
JEAN *inside his cabin.*
JULIETTE *in the ferry.*
JEAN *getting ready for bed. He undresses. Before getting into*
bed, he stares in front of him.
JULIETTE, *in her bedroom, is undressing.*
JEAN, *in bed.*
JULIETTE, *in bed.*

JEAN	⎫	*In their respective beds* JEAN *and*
JULIETTE	⎬	JULIETTE *move about as to suggest that*
JEAN		*they are actually lying in the same bed*
JULIETTE	⎭	*together.*

JEAN *gets up and lights a cigarette.*
The barge arriving at Le Havre. PÈRE JULES *is at the helm.*
L'Atalante advancing in Le Havre harbour, along with other
barges and large cargo boats.
THE KID, *watching.*

PÈRE JULES *shouting to* THE KID: Go tell the boss we're coming
into Le Havre.

JEAN *emerges from his cabin, thin and unshaven. He hops off the barge onto the quayside.* PÈRE JULES *follows him.*
JEAN *walking along the quay.*
JEAN *in the harbour near some ships.*
JEAN *walking. People turning to stare at him.*
JEAN *on the breakwater, facing the sea. He starts running wildly in the direction of the sea, then stops and turns back, slowly walking towards the quay, a despondent expression on his face.*
JEAN *staggers and collapses on a bollard. People cluster round him.*
People milling round JEAN *who sits holding his head in his hands.*

A MAN: Another drunken sailor. It's a disgrace.

PÈRE JULES *comes forward and glares at the man who has just spoken. The man makes himself scarce and the others follow suit.*
Shot of crowd dispersing.
JEAN *goes on sitting on the bollard. He has not registered what was going on around him.* PÈRE JULES *taps him on the shoulder; the two men look at one another and then leave together.*
JEAN *and* PÈRE JULES *returning to l'Atalante together.*
A transatlantic liner steaming out of harbour.
L'Atalante on the move. PÈRE JULES *is at the helm;* JEAN *is lying on the deck.*
A sailing boat.
Barges on the river.
Ships on the sea.
Barges.
L'Atalante moored at the spot where JULIETTE *ran away.* PÈRE JULES *and* THE KID *are on the deck.* JEAN *emerges from his cabin, unshaven.*

PÈRE JULES: Well, you got dressed at least, but you should have shaved too. The head of the Company Office wants to see us. *(to* THE KID*)* See you this evening.

JEAN *and* PÈRE JULES *leave.* THE KID *stays behind on l'Atalante.*

147

THE KID: Good luck.
PÈRE JULES: Shut up, will you?

Office of the Company to which l'Atalante belongs. Sailors are waiting about in the corridor, outside the PERSONNEL MANAGER'S *office. The* MANAGER *is talking to one of the Company employees, who stands on the threshold of the office.*

MANAGER: You had no business taking the matter into your own hands. Who do you think you are, anyway?
EMPLOYEE: Me? I'm a nobody.
MANAGER: A nobody, are you?
EMPLOYEE: Yes, a nobody.
MANAGER: A nobody! Well, if that's all you are, then go and pick up your wage packet and push off.

We can still hear the MANAGER'S *voice as* PÈRE JULES *and* JEAN *come into shot.*

MANAGER'S VOICE: And where's the captain of l'Atalante? It won't take long to settle matters with him either, now he's in harbour. (JEAN *sits down and* PÈRE JULES *looks towards the* MANAGER'S *office as camera pans in that direction.*) Ah! There you are! You, over there. Yes, you, the boatswain of l'Atalante. Come over here. Yes, by yourself.

PÈRE JULES *hesitates, taps* JEAN *on the shoulder to urge him to follow, then enters the office alone. The camera tracks after him into the* MANAGER'S *office.*

MANAGER: Shut the door. I haven't any time to waste.

PÈRE JULES *closes the door.*
JEAN *sitting in the corridor. The employee who has been fired is pocketing his wage envelope. He calls out to* JEAN.

EMPLOYEE: A nobody, that's what I am. They're right. We're nobodies. Waiting for your turn, are you? Well, better hurry. The pay counter shuts at noon.

Inside the office. The MANAGER, *an employee and* PÈRE JULES.

MANAGER: Is the captain of l'Atalante doing his job or isn't he?

148

What's all this evidence that's been collected about him? Means nothing, does it?

PÈRE JULES: Doesn't mean much at any rate. Mainly gossip, I'd say.

MANAGER: You claim he's doing his job properly on l'Atalante? Watch it, now, or it may cost you a pretty penny. Won't be the first time *you've* got into trouble.

PÈRE JULES: I ought to know what's going on, oughtn't I? I could tell you a thing or two myself.

MANAGER: Don't you get smart! Is the captain of l'Atalante doing his job or isn't he?

PÈRE JULES: If he weren't, who'd be doing it in his place? I haven't got a license and it ain't the kid who can get the barge to move by blowing on it! If you ask me, all those stories going round are a load of baloney.

MANAGER: All right, we'll see to it another time. I've got work to do. L'Atalante isn't the only boat in the world. You just sort things out with your boss.

JEAN, *sitting in the corridor. The office door opens and* PÈRE JULES *emerges. He drags* JEAN *off with him.*

MANAGER'S Voice: It's unbelievable! Who do you take me for? That file's none of my business. Toss it in the waste-paper basket.

Pan to office. The MANAGER *addresses himself to another boatsman who is waiting in the corridor.*

MANAGER: So you're the captain of 'La Belle Amélie' are you? Come in, Loiselet. I've had about enough. It won't take a minute, you just see.

The boatsman goes into the office and the MANAGER *shuts the door behind him.*

JEAN *and* PÈRE JULES *returning to l'Atalante.* THE KID *is waiting for them.* JEAN *goes straight to his cabin and shuts himself in.*

PÈRE JULES *and* THE KID *alone on the upper deck.*

PÈRE JULES: The boss almost got fired by the Company. It can't go on like this. I'm going looking for the missus.

THE KID: You're going to hunt down the missus, are you?

PÈRE JULES: You bet I am. Just look at the state the boss is in. I'll leave you in charge. Are you up to it?
THE KID: Am I up to it!
PÈRE JULES: Right! I'm off then, and I'll come back with the missus, I can tell you.

PÈRE JULES *jumps off l'Atalante.*

THE KID: What! You're leaving right away?
PÈRE JULES: Well, I'm not going to wait till the 14th of July!

JEAN *inside his cabin.*
PÈRE JULES *crossing a bridge then stopping short in his tracks.*

 *

A woman has been knocked over by a car. An ambulance arrives on the scene. PÈRE JULES comes into shot and tries to get a better look. The woman is carried past on a stretcher. PÈRE JULES sighs with relief upon seeing that it is not JULIETTE. He goes off again.

PÈRE JULES, *sitting on a bench in a public park. Then walking down a street and stopping before a shop window.*
Shot of a woman standing on a step-ladder, cleaning the shop-window.
The woman half turns round. It is JULIETTE.
PÈRE JULES *peers at her.*
The woman has turned right round. It is not JULIETTE after all.
PÈRE JULES *stops again, a worried look on his face. He has heard a beggar woman calling out in JULIETTE'S voice:*

BEGGAR WOMAN: Please, sir, charity if you please.

PÈRE JULES *takes a closer look at the woman. It is not JULIETTE.*
JULIETTE, *inside a shop which sells music-boxes. She is dusting the music-boxes and stops in front of one which is labelled*

---

* Not included in the final version.

*'Song of the Boatmen'. She steals a glance in the direction of the
cash register.*
The shop owner, nodding off in front of his cash register.
JULIETTE *hastily slips a counter into the music-box and picks
up the earphone. We hear the Boatmen's Song throughout the
following shots.*
PÈRE JULES *stops in front of the boatsmen's café where we once
saw* JULIETTE *enter. He cocks an ear.*
PÈRE JULES *walks down the street, trying to ascertain where the
music he hears is coming from. He stops again.*
The shop which sells music-boxes. The loud-speaker.
Close-up of the loud-speaker.
JULIETTE, *standing in front of the mirror of a music-box; she is
listening to the Boatmen's Song. She hears* JEAN'S *voice calling
out to her. Suddenly,* PÈRE JULES'S *face appears next to hers in
the mirror. She reels backwards.*
PÈRE JULES *grabs* JULIETTE *and carries her off bodily as
people look on, staring and following them.*
JEAN *and* THE KID *inside the cabin.*

JEAN: Père Jules went to fetch the missus?
THE KID: Yep. He knows where she is.
JEAN: Do you promise he'll bring her back?

He rushes over to a mirror which hangs on the wall.

THE KID: Yep.

JEAN, *standing in front of the mirror.*

JEAN: Go fetch me some water.

THE KID *dashes out of the cabin, carrying an empty bucket.*
JEAN *starts undressing.*
THE KID *up on deck, drawing water.*
Inside the cabin. THE KID *returns and* JEAN *starts to wash.*
THE KID, *heating up the water.*
JEAN, *washing.* THE KID *finishes tidying up, then leaves.*
JEAN *washing.*
THE KID, *up on deck, acting as lookout.*
JEAN, *shaving in the cabin.*
THE KID, *watching.*

THE KID, *shouting*: Here they come!

PÈRE JULES *and* JULIETTE *on the towpath, close to the barge.*
THE KID, *leaning down and yelling to* JEAN *inside the cabin:*

THE KID: The missus and Père Jules are coming!

JEAN, *who has only just finished washing, tidies up hastily.*
JEAN *adopts a frowning expression as he prepares to go up on deck. Suddenly, we see* JULIETTE'S *legs appear on the steps. She comes down into the cabin.*
JEAN *steps back.*
JEAN *and* JULIETTE, *standing face to face, embarrassed.*
We hear the noise of l'Atalante's engine starting up. JEAN *and* JULIETTE *smile as they hear the sound and fall into each other's arms. They fall to the ground, locked in an embrace, overjoyed.*
Fade to aerial view of:
L'Atalante moving forward, then pan beyond it to the river itself.

END

FILMOGRAPHY

1929 – *A PROPOS DE NICE* (short)
Subtitled: *Point de Vue Documenté*
Directed by: Jean Vigo
Photography: Boris Kaufman
First private screening at the Théâtre du Vieux-Colombier, 28 May, 1930.
Second screening at the Vieux-Colombier organised by the *Groupement des Spectateurs d'Avant-Garde*. Vigo introduced the film himself in an informal speech entitled: *Vers un Cinéma Social*.
The film had a brief showing at the Ursulines Cinema (September–October 1930), then went on release to various film clubs.

1931 – *TARIS OU LA NATATION* (short)
Also entitled: *TARIS, ROI DE L'EAU*.
First documentary produced by the *Journal Vivant* (artistic director: C. Morskoï)
Written and directed by: Jean Vigo.
Photography: Boris Kaufman.
Shot at the Sporting swimming-pool (Rue de l'Elysée, Paris)

1933 – *ZERO DE CONDUITE*
Producer: J.L. Nounez, for Argui-Films
Scenario, dialogue and direction: Jean Vigo
Photography: Boris Kaufman, assisted by Louis Berger
Assistant directors: Albert Riéra and Pierre Merle
Assistant producer: Henri Storck
Songs: Charles Goldblatt

Music: Maurice Jaubert
Sound: Royné and Bocquel
Make-up: Massard
Shooting schedule: 24 December, 1932 – 22 January, 1933
Locations: Saint-Cloud and the railway station of the Beleville – La Villette Loop
Studio: Buttes-Chaumont
Length: 47 minutes (1200 metres)
Cast:

> Jean Dasté: *Schoolmaster Huguet*
> Robert Le Flon: *Schoolmaster Parrain ('Pète-Sec')*
> Delphin: *Headmaster*
> Du Verron: *A Schoolmaster*
> Blanchar: *The Vice-Principal ('Bec de gaz')*
> Léon Larive: *The Chemistry Teacher*
> Louis Berger: *Friend acting as a Parent*
> Louis de Gonzague-Frick: *Prefect*
> Henri Storck: *A Priest*
> Félix Labisse: *First Fireman*
> Georges Patin: *Second Fireman*
> Raphaël Diligent: *Third Fireman*
> Georges Vakalo: *Fourth Fireman*
> Mme Emile: *Ma Bean*
> Michelle Fagard: *The Little Girl*
> Albert Riéra: *Night Watchman*
> Louis Lefèbvre: *Caussat*
> Gilbert Pruchon: *Colin*
> Gérard de Bedarieux: *Tabard*
> Constantin Kelber: *Bruel*
>
> Georges Belmer, Emile Boulez, Maurice Cariel, Jean-Pierre Dumesnil, Igor Goldfarb, Lucien Lincks, Charles Michels, Roger Porte, Jacques Poulin, Pierre Regnoux, Ali Ronchy, Georges Rougette, André Thille, Pierre Tridon, Paul Vilhem: *Children*
> Natale Bencini and Leonello Bencini played the role of children in certain acrobatic scenes.

1934 – *L'ATALANTE*

Producer: J.L. Nounez
Distributor: Gaumont-Franco-Film-Aubert
Scenario and dialogue: Jean Vigo and Albert Riéra, from a work by J. Guinée (R. de Guichen)
Directed by: Jean Vigo
Photography: Boris Kaufman, assisted by Louis Berger and Jean Paul Alphen
Sets: Francis Jourdain
Music: Maurice Jaubert
Songs: Charles Goldblatt
Editing: Louis Chavance
Script Boy: Fred Matter
Recording: Radio-Cinéma
Location: Conflans, Ste. Honorine and Maurecourt (Oise), and a number of canals and rivers in the Ile de France (Oise, Seine, Canal de l'Ourcq, Canal St Martin, Bassin de la Villette), Paris.
Studio: G.F.F., Buttes-Chaumont
Length: 89 minutes
First screening: 24 April, 1934
World Première: Colisée cinema, September 1934

Cast:

Michel Simon: *Père Jules*
Jean Dasté: *Jean, Captain of L'Atalante*
Dita Parlo: *Jean's Wife, Juliette*
Gilles Margaritis: *Travelling Salesman*
Louis Lefebvre: *The Kid*
Fanny Clar: *Juliette's Mother*
Raphaël Diligent: *Tramp*
René Block, Gen-Paul, Charles Goldblatt, Pierre Prévert: *various small parts or extras*

The distributors insisted that *L'ATALANTE* be renamed *LE CHALAND QUI PASSE*, from the title of a successful song by C.A. Bixio which was inserted in the film. The actual release of the film with its proper title and in the form planned by Vigo did not occur until October 1940, when it was shown for three weeks at the Studio des Ursulines.

155

NOTE: Jean Vigo left four screenplays written by himself
which he did not film. They were entitled: *Lourdes,
Lignes de la Main, Chauvinisme,* and *Au Café.*

Vigo also hoped to film eight screenplays by other
writers. These were *L'Evadé du Bagne* (J. Dupont–
E. Dieudonné), *L'Execution de Marinèche* and *Le
Timide Qui Prend Feu* (C. Aveline), *Matineé* (L.
Levy and H. Storck), *La Déesse* (F. Labisse),
L'Inventeur (A. Riéra), *M. Evariste* (H. Storck), and
Si On Pariait (J. Supervielle).